Digging for Buried Treasure:

52 Prop-Based Play Therapy Interventions For Treating the Problems of Childhood

Written by:
Paris Goodyear-Brown, LCSW, RPT-S

Resources and upcoming workshop information can be found at **www.parisandme.com**.
For supervision, consultation or training, send e-mail to **paris@parisandme.com** *or contact by phone at* **615-397-9480**.

Table of Contents

Introduction

This treatment manual represents all the wonderful gifts given to me over the years by my child clients: the gifts of creation, the gifts of mutual collaboration in the journey towards growth and wholeness. Most of the techniques described here evolved directly out of various treatment sessions. In these sessions, a child would get to a certain plateau in understanding and working through the issues that brought him to therapy. An intervention was then created as a desperate measure to push the client deeper into the work of therapy. It will not suprise those of you who do the majority of your work with children that this "jumpstart" almost always came through fun and unexpected uses of play materials. The techniques are broken down into categories based on the area of skill building that needs to be addressed. They are not broken down according to specific diagnoses because many of the same emotional and psychological challenges as well as skills deficits are faced by children across symptom clusters. Social skills, anger management skills, self-esteem builders, coping strategies and avenues for feelings expression are arenas in which our clients need training, regardless of their diagnoses.

I have labeled the techniques in this book "prop-based" because each technique utilizes a prop of some sort. I have found the use of concrete items in treatment to be invaluable. The props serve several functions. First and most importantly, props serve to break through the resistance of child clients. They often come to therapy believing that they are going to have to "talk" or "perform". When a prop is placed in their hands, the worry of having to talk the whole session is alleviated. The introduction of the object also gives the child an excuse to break eye contact that can be intimidating during the initial relationship bulding phase of treatment. Second, the prop often serves to concretize or carry a metaphoric message related to a concept such as anger or fear and allows for work to be done consciously and unconsciously at the same time. Third, the props often serve as a vehicle for externalizing a problem or issue that the child is facing. Once the problem has been put outside the child, the child is better equipped to analyze it and to generate solutions or coping strategies to deal with it. Fourth, research into neurolinguistics tells us that children have different learning styles (auditory, visual, kinesthetic or a combination of these). Using props allows for kinesthetic learning to occur and can augment visual and auditory processes that are taking place in the playroom. Finally, it's just plain fun to play with props. Children can work on even the most difficult problems while having a parallel experience that naturally creates enjoyment.

Many therapists have natural gifts for working with children. Creating new play therapy activities comes easily to many. Others prefer to use previously created interventions from books and spend their energies molding the exercises to their client populations. Please let me stress that no intervention should ever be pulled out of a hat or even this book without giving careful consideration to the client's needs, the treatment goals and the placement of the intervention in the continuum of the therapeutic process. For you creative types, this book will likely spark a whole new batch of your own interventions. For those of you who call yourself "creatively challenged", you will adapt these techniques to your own special way of being with children. For all of you, the techniques are broken down into sub-sections for easy reference.

Treatment Modality: This section gives you a quick glance at the treatment settings in which this technique might be most appropriate. Some techniques are more suited for work with individuals while others are more appropriate for group or family work. Most of the techniques could be modified to work in any of these treatment milieues.

Population: The age range of who may benefit from the intervention is listed here. Be aware that the developmental age is a more relevant guide than chronological age.

Treatment Phase: This section helps you to place the intervention within the therapeutic process. These stages are loosely broken down into the initial or joining phase in which relationship is building and trust is being established; the middle or working phase in which the meat of treatment is occurring; and the termination or ending phase of treatment in which previous work is being integrated and client's are saying goodbye.

Props: This section details the materials that you will need to complete each activity.

Procedure: This section gives a step by step guide for the clinician detailing how to orchestrate the intervention.

Processing Questions: This section lists questions that the clinician may use to process the intervention after it is complete and to deepen the client's awareness or therapeutic learning.

Homework assignment: This section gives a homework assignment for the client. The homework helps crystallize new concepts, practice new skills and gain new experiences that strengthen the therapeutic work being done in session. Homework assigments may need to be modified according to the age and capacities of the child.

Special considerations: This section will sometimes describe populations with which the intervention may be more or less effective, adaptations to be made for children with various challenges and general "watch outs" that have grown out of this therapist's repeated completion of these interventions with clients.

Applications and modifications: This section often delineates alternative settings in which the intervention can be used. If the procedures described above were geared for work with an individual client, this section may discuss ways in which the technique can be modified for use in groups.

Many clinicians have asked how I generate these ideas. The answer is not complicated. I let the prop guide me. I ask myself how a particular tool could be helpful in communicating a therapeutic metaphor or teaching a therapeutic skill. I ask myself, "What is the function for which this object exists?" For a set of magnifying glasses, the answer is "to magnify things...to make certain images larger". Then I ask myself what parts of a child's life need to be magnified. Most children who come to therapy have low self-esteem and tend to see and hear the negative statements people make about them more clearly than the positive ones. Out of this train of thought came the technique, "Magnifying the Feel Goods". Try out the process on your own and soon you'll have a whole new repertoire of interventions. In closing, I would like to address the title of this book. Each child that we see has inside himself a treasure trove of riches. Many times the child needs help finding these beautiful gems within himself. It is my hope that careful application of the techniques enumerated in this text will result in uncovering the buried treasure within the children we serve.

Tools
for Use
in
Gathering
Information

The Preschool Play Geno-game

Treatment Modality: Individual/Group
Population: Ages 3 to 12
Treatment Phase: Beginning/Assessment

Treatment Goals:

1. To assess client's self-perception of family dynamics
2. To build relationship
3. To assess client's ability to focus and complete tasks
4. To assess client's imaginative capacities

Props:

white butcher paper
markers
tokens or treasures
lots of toys to choose from (the choices are not limited to traditional items used in sandtray work)

Procedure:

This technique is a modification of the ground breaking work done by Eliana Gil around Family Play Genograms. This technique sets up the creation of the genogram as a game with incentives, a built-in token economy system, and a follow-up storytelling technique. This adaptation of a traditional assessment tool adds to the layers of assessment information that may be gained with very young children. This game was first designed for preschool age children. These children do not yet have the words to articulate even the behaviors that they observe in their family members, much less how their observations have shaped their idealization of each member of the family. The addition of the play figures to represent each family member offers an outlet through which these children can give clear descriptions in their own language. Begin by drawing the client's genogram on a large sheet of butcher paper. Explain that a "map" of his family is being drawn. Encourage the client to help you with names and ages of family members and be sure that all family members whom the client considers important are included. Clients may include a great-grandmother, an aunt or a pet. The information is likely to be inaccurate - I've had clients tell me that their parents are twelve and their brother is fifty. The reliability of the information is less important than the feeling the child has that he is helping to create his own family map. This sense of ownership increases the client's motivation to complete the activity. Once the map is complete, place a stone or treasure on each circle and square that represents a family member. Then give this direction: "This is a game in which you get to pick any toy in the whole room to be your mom. Go get the toy. When you bring it back and put it on the paper, you get to take the stone and put it in your cup. When you have gathered all five stones (this number will vary with the number of family members) you can trade in the stones for a treasure. Ready? Go find a toy to be your mom." When the child has chosen a toy to represent each family member and has placed it on the genogram, invite the client to tell a story about the symbols on the "map". At the end of the activity the client trades in all of his tokens for a reward.

3

Processing Questions:

Tell me a story about these characters.
Is there another ending that you would like to give your story?
How does each character feel about being part of this family?
What is one thing each character worries about? Wishes for?
Is there any character that you would like to change or replace with another toy? Why?

Homework Assignment:

This is a tool for gathering information. Moreover, when dealing with preschool age children it is usually ineffective to assign homework, therefore no homework assignment accompanies this technique.

Special Considerations:

The youngest children may need verbal reminder prompts to go and get the next figure after the last figure has been placed. When the storytelling phase of the technique is happening, it is crucial to help the client stay in the metaphors. The easiest way to accomplish this goal is to have the client use the names (or create names) for the characters. Therefore, the story would begin, "Once upon a time Snow White...", as opposed to "Once upon a time, mom...". The more layers of removal the client feels from the scene she has created, the more unguarded perceptions and projective information you will be able to glean about the client's perceptions of his family dynamics.

Applications and Modifications:

In terms of assessment, it is important to look not only at what figure the child chooses, but at how the child chooses it. For example, one client immediately picked up a terrifying looking alien to be his father, but then put it back and chose a superhero instead. Children may reveal themselves symbolically or they may create a "model" family that evidences their denial of dysfunctional family patterns. A four year old chose three different figures to be Dad and placed them all on the genogram together. One figure was a large, very aggressive looking wrestler, another was a small, inconsequential looking male figure who could not stand up on his own, and the third was Phoebus, the kindly prince from the Disney movie, The Hunchback of Notre Dame. This child had witnessed the domestic violence cycle and was describing the three stages in his choice of the three figures. I have used this same technique in groups of children. Each member draws a genogram and completes the activity. Group members then tell their stories to the whole group. Older children often want to explain their choice of characters more overtly and I allow them to do so. The therapist can also use the technique to assess the client's attentional abilities. Can he focus on the search for a toy to represent the mother, or is he sidetracked by other toys? Can he remember where it goes on the genogram? The way in which the child approaches this task may reflect difficulties that he has in other life arenas.

Color Your Heart

Treatment Modality: Individual/Group
Population: Ages 3 to adult
Treatment Phase: Beginning (also Working/Termination)

Treatment Goals:

1. To assess the extent of the client's emotional vocabulary.
2. To assess the client's self-perception of her emotional life.
3. To target feelings that need particular therapeutic intervention (sadness, anger, loneliness)

Props:

blank paper
crayons or markers

Procedure:

This technique is a modification of Kevin O'Connor's Color Your Life Technique. Begin by explaining that every person has many feelings all stored inside of her at the same time. Draw a large heart on a blank sheet of paper. Then draw blank boxes that represent the color code in the bottom right hand corner of the page. Help the client choose what color will represent what feeling for him during this activity. This is important because although it may seem intuitive that blue equals sad, a particular client might have a different color/feeling association. Having a predetermined color grid may limit the value of the assessment tool. The client should choose at least five feeling words and match them with colors (the therapist can do the writing for very young children). Give the client the following prompt: "Color in as much of the heart as you want for each color in your color grid. Try to match the amount of the color that you put inside the heart to the amount of each feeling that is in your heart right now . For example, if the client chooses red to represent feeling angry and she colors in a lot of red, this will reflect the fact that the client feels very angry right now.

Processing Questions:
What were the first feeling words that you thought of?
What are some feelings that are absent from this drawing (i.e. your heart)?
Are there any colors/feelings that you would like to add to or take away from your heart?
How would you like your heart to look in six months? A year?

Homework Assignment:
Be aware that the therapist will keep this picture in your special book. Be prepared to color a new heart after you have worked together with the therapist for awhile.

Special Considerations:
Very young clients may have trouble remembering which color represents which feeling, even though they made the pairings themselves. The therapist may want to start with the first color on the color grid and give the prompt "This color is yellow and you decided that it means happy. Color in as much happy as is in your own heart today." Wait until the client is finished before moving on to the next color and feeling.

Applications and Modifications:

This is a fun and quick way to get affective information about a client at any point in therapy. I usually do one heart with clients at the beginning of therapy and then another in the middle or at the end. In most cases, the client and I are both gratified to see that the number of colors/feelings have increased, evidencing the client's growing awareness of the vast array of feelings she carries inside. Moreover, the difficult emotions that have dominated (such as anger, fear, sadness) have usually decreased. Many times the client does not accurately remember her first drawing, which makes the comparison especially rewarding. Occasionally, the second drawing will highlight for the therapist the fact that a new treatment issue has arisen. For instance, the client may no longer have as much fear of the perpetrator, but may be brimming over with sadness or anger). This modification of the Color Your Life technique differs from O'Connor's work in two main ways. First, the client chooses the pairings of affect and color in this technique. Second this technique is not intended to review or identify all of the feelings that have experienced previously, but more immediately, what her affective states are at the present time. It is meant to be used as a self-report assessment measure. You could use this technique to track clients through the grieving process, to make parents more clearly aware of the emotional life of their child and to direct your own treatment planning.

Color Your Heart
(examples)

The following "Color Your Heart" picture was drawn by a four year old girl shortly after she entered treatment. The feelings represented here are (from left to right) angry, silly, disappointed, sad and embarrassed. The brown patch in the top right hand corner is "noisy" and the very small yellow portion is happy.

This "Color Your Heart" drawing was done by the same child much later in the therapy process. Notice the proliferation of feelings vocabulary and colored portions of the heart. This heart reflects the clients development of awareness of a wider array of feelings, as well as a shrinking of the feelings of anger, disappointment that had monopolized her emotional life at the beginning of treatment. Notice also how much larger her yellow (happy) patch has become.

9

King of Nashville

Treatment Modality: Individual/Group/Family
Population: Ages 6 to 12
Treatment Phase: Beginning/ Assessment

Treatment Goals:
1. To gather assessment information
2. To investigate client's sense of right and wrong
3. To explore areas of the client's life over which he would like more control

Props:
plastic king's crown
plush king's hat
scepter
cape (or sheet)
paper
markers

Procedure:
My office space is on the twelfth floor of a building that overlooks downtown Nashville. Often, when a new child client comes to see me for the first time, she goes straight to the window and says something like "Wow, you can see the whole

city from here." I make an invitation by saying, "Let's pretend that you are the King (or Queen) of Nashville." I give them a crown (or the plush king's hat), a scepter, maybe even a cape. I get a piece of paper and a pen and I kneel before the client, saying "Oh, wise King. You are the master of all you survey. What are going to be the laws of the land, the rules of your Kingdom?" The client usually giggles and enjoys being put in this esteemed position. The client then generates three of four rules or laws. After the exercise is over, I ask if the client would like any of the laws that he created as the "King of Nashville" to actually exist in her own life. Lastly, I ask the client to draw a picture of what his Kingdom would look like if everyone obeyed his laws. Clients will often give you valuable information about their wishes, hopes and worries through the laws they create. The first law created by one of my eight year old girls was "There shall be NO SMOKING in Nashville." She was terrified that her mother was going to die from lung cancer. Another client decided that no divorce would be allowed in his Kingdom. You can guess the issues for which he came to therapy. The laws that clients generate give you some insight into their moral development and their sense of right and wrong. At the same time, the laws help the therapist pinpoint life issues for further exploration.

Processing Questions:
What is the most important law in your Kingdom?
What do you think your subjects would do if you didn't make the laws?
How does it feel to be the King and make the laws?
How will the laws get enforced in your Kingdom?
Who is most likely to break the law?

Homework Assignment:
Pick one of the laws of your Kingdom and tell it to your parents or caregivers. Find out what their laws would be if they were the King and queen of Nashville.

Special Considerations:

Make sure that the parents understand the point of this exercise before you have the client complete the homework assignment. Some parents might feel very threatened by their child's laws, especially if the child's law concerned putting a limitation on a parent's behavior. The therapist may have to guide the child through the process of deciding which law (wish or hope) he should share with his parent.

Applications and Modifications:

This technique is a wonderful way to empower children while building the initial relationship with the therapist. Normally, this technique is done during the assessment period with an individual client (along with other projective techniques like the K-F-D, three wishes and other techniques from the assessment section of this book). However, the technique could be done in a group or family setting. In this case, each group or family member would get a chance to be the King and make up laws for the Kingdom. These laws would then be read to the rest of the group or family, and the group together would choose one law from each person's list. In this way, everyone would contribute to the laws of the land. This technique can also be adapted to help a client work on boundary issues. For example, the therapist could help the client generate and practice healthy laws for touching, for expressing anger, etc.

The view of Nashville (the child's Kingdom) seen from the office window.

Edible Animal Farm

Treatment Modality: Individual/Group/Family
Population: Ages 3 to adults
Treatment Phase: Beginning phase

Treatment Goals:

1. To assess family dynamics
2. To explore client's perception of family relationships
3. To engage in treatment planning regarding client and family relationships
4. To indirectly nurture client (through food)
5. To establish rapport and build relationship with the therapist

Props:

graham crackers
peanut butter
animal crackers

Procedure:

This technique is projective in nature. The metaphor of animals is used to get at the underlying dynamics in the client's family of origin and/or the client's nuclear family (these may or may not be the same). Take several graham crackers and lay them side by side on a flat surface. Give the client peanut butter and explain that this will act as mortar to attach the graham crackers to each other. Help the client spread peanut butter across the top of the graham cracker "plate" to provide a sticky base for the animal crackers. When this step is finished, present the client with several different kinds of animal crackers. Examples include well defined animals, less defined animals, and icing covered animals. Prompt the client to choose an animal cracker to represent each family member. This is why it is important to have several different varieties of animal cracker. Once the child has chosen an animal for each parent, ask her to pretend that they live on a farm together. Instruct the client to arrange the animals "on the farm" doing something together. When the client is finished, have her make up a story about the animals on the farm. Present the following rules to the client: The story must have a beginning, a middle, and an end. All the characters on the farm must be mentioned at some point in the story. The client can make the farm as fancy as she wants, depending on what you have available. She may want to add a fence to function as a boundary or green coconut for grass. Try to have many options available to her.

Processing Questions:

Which animal do you like the most? The least? Why?

I'm going to read the story back to you. How do different characters in the story feel?

Would any of the animals leave the farm if they could? Which ones, and why?

Take each animal, one by one, and describe it using as many adjectives as you can.

If your farm could be changed in some way, how would you change it? (After taking a picture of the first farm, allow them to change it.)

Homework Assignment:

This week, look for one way that each of your family members acts like the animal that you chose for him or her. Be prepared to talk about this during your next session.

Special Considerations:

Food based interventions may not be appropriate for children with eating disorders or children suffering from obesity. The youngest children may need a prompt with each family member, like "Pick an animal to be your mom." They may also need more prompts during the story, such as "and then what happened?" or "What does the elephant do in your story?"

Applications and Modifications:

The Edible Animal Farm is a fun way to help a child client explore her perceptions of her family dynamics while nurturing her through the use of food. This technique may be particularly helpful to do with adopted children and children with divorced or remarried families. When a child has two homes, an animal farm is done for each. The story may then involve how the two farms relate to each other as well as how the animals within each farm relate to each other. In an adoption situation, the child may or may not want to include birth parents or foster family members to whom the child became attached. Children will sometimes ask for extra graham crackers and make little islands, where animals (family members) are physically removed from the nuclear family.

The therapist can process the animal farm with the client in much the same way that a sandtray would be processed. How close together or far apart are family members? Are they facing each other or are their backs turned? Are there alliances? Are there outcasts? How does it feel to be a particular animal on the farm?

After the farm has been processed in its initial construction, it is important to give the client an opportunity to change it and to make psychological meaning of the visual changes.   For instance, the therapist might invite the client to change the farm in some way, and the client moves the animal representing mom closer to the client's own animal.   The client should be encouraged to experience what feelings the visual change stimulates and to make the psychological connection that she desires deeper intimacy with mom.

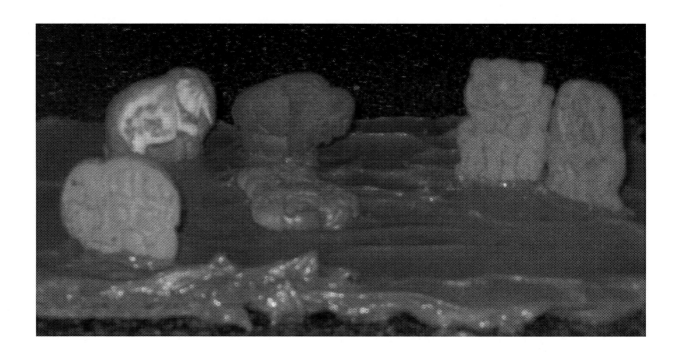

This is an example of how a client's animal farm might look.   The mother is the iced elephant "because she always dresses nice".   The father is standing beside the mother (which may signify a strong parental unit or an exclusion of the children).   The father is a lion, "because he's always roaring at us".   In the back right hand corner are a kitty cat and a puppy.   These represent the client's twin siblings "because they're real cute and always together".   In the middle, laying down, is the new baby, represented by a cuddly teddy bear.   The identified client (shown at the bottom left corner of the picture, chooses a turtle to represent himself "because I'm real slow at school".   Notice how isolated the turtle is from the rest of the animals.

Head In The Clouds

Treatment Modality: Individual/Group/Family
Population: Ages 3 to 10
Treatment Phase: Beginning (also Working/Termination)

Treatment Goals:
1. To gather assessment information
2. To explore client's wishes and dreams
3. To explore client's sense of self

Props:
Little Cloud by Eric Carle, and/or
It Looked Like Spilt Milk by Charles G. Shaw
whipped cream (shaving cream can be substituted)
aprons/smocks

Procedure:
Begin by reading Little Cloud. The book is about a little cloud that drifts away from the rest of the clouds and takes on various shapes of things that it has seen (examples include a shark, a clown, a hat). One excerpt reads as follows: "Little Cloud turned into two trees because he like the way that trees never moved and always stayed in one place." The story itself includes the metaphor of change and also helps children understand that it is O.K. to fantasize about being things that you are not. Little Cloud ends up rejoining all the big clouds at

the end of the story. <u>It Looked Like Spilt Milk</u> is another children's book in which a cloud looks like different objects on different pages and may be used as an additional resource during the activity. After reading the story, give the client a smock and a container of whipped cream. The cans are especially good for this exercise. They can be aimed and clients can draw with the stream of whipped cream. Ask the child to imagine what she would want to be (what shape she would want to take) if she were a cloud. When the child has finished creating her whipped cream cloud shape, instruct the client to create a story about her cloud.

Processing Questions:
What were the different shapes that went through your head before you chose one?
List some words that describe your cloud shape.
How did the whipped cream feel on your hands?
How did it feel to be messy?
Is there any way in which you would like to change your cloud now?
For groups, What was it like to combine your shape with others and make a new cloud?

Homework Assignment:
Spend some time laying down and looking up at the clouds in the sky. Bring back a list of all the shapes that you could see in the clouds.

Special Considerations:
Older children might find the books "childish", so be sure you know your population before you use this technique. Again, because it involves food, this technique might not be appropriate for children with eating disorders. The technique involves fantasy and projection and may not be appropriate for children who have difficulties with reality testing (i.e. psychosis). The tactile component of the exercise (touching and

manipulating the cold, wet, whipped cream) might *be* a trigger for certain children who have experienced sexual abuse. Therefore, relaxation training and strong trust in the therapist are pre-requisites for using this technique with survivors of sexual abuse.

Applications and Modifications:

This technique can *be* done with individual children and may *be* particularly fun in a family session or a group setting. In the group or family setting, each participant would make his/her own cloud shape. However, the story that each member creates would have to tie in all of the cloud shapes created. After everyone has had a chance to tell their story, the therapist can direct the members to push all of the whipped cream into the middle of the space and create one cloud shape all together. This is a great cooperation building activity.

Another therapeutic component to this activity is that it involves the senses. Clients get their hands dirty and are kinesthetically involved at the same time that they are creating a fantastical cloud shape and story. Besides, using whipped cream is just fun!

This technique can *be* used to expand a client's repertoire of relaxation exercises. The therapist can encourage the client to close her eyes while listening to the stories and imagine herself becoming each of those shapes (this is a form of guided imagery). The client could then practice bringing up these images again in stressful situations. Moreover, if there is time in the session to go outside, lay down and look up at the clouds, this is intrinsically relaxing. The same thing can *be* done in the child's imagination by just having them lay down in the office, or the therapist could even cut out various cloud shapes in white paper and put them on the ceiling.

This technique could *be* used during the termination phase with the prompt, "Create a cloud shape that shows how you want the group (or therapist) to remember you."

Head In The Clouds
(an example)

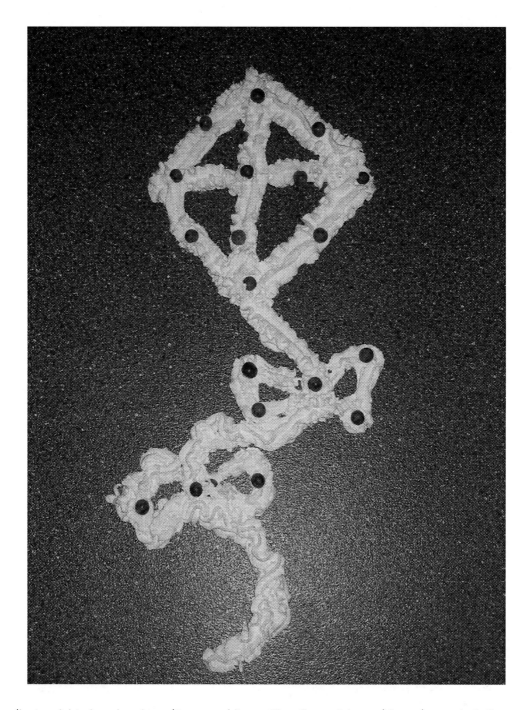

A client might imagine herself as a kite. The therapist would explore what it means to the client to be a kite. It might represent lightness or freedom or beauty to the client. The client then has a concrete image to bring back up when trying to relax.

20

Feelings Expression and Verbalization

Rice Cake Feeling Faces

Treatment Modality: Individual/Group/Family
Population: Ages 3 to adult
Treatment Phase: Beginning/Working/Termination   phase

Treatment Goals:

1.   To correctly pair physical affect with feelings
2.   To identify feelings
3.   To expand feelings vocabulary

Props:

rice cakes
icing (in several colors)
peanut butter
candies,
dried fruits
peanuts

Procedure:

This technique is a modification of an idea created by a graduate student of mine, Tracy Steyer. Present the client with a rice cake and explain that the client is going to create a series of rice cake feeling faces, based on a story that will be read. Choose whatever bibiliotherapy material is appropriate for the child's clinical issues. It is usually a good idea to create the first one together. "Happy" is the least threatening feeling for most children, so this is a good one to use as the example. Begin by choosing a color of icing or peanut butter (it is important to have vanilla, milk chocolate, caramel and dark chocolate so that different skin colors can be represented). Have mini M&M's available for eyes, dried apricots or Twizzlers for a mouth, gum drops for a nose, dried apples for ears, etc. The more edible accessories that are available, the more detailed the client's face will be. Once the example is complete begin telling the story. Challenge the client to raise his hand each time that the main character in the story has a different feeling. Whenever a new feeling seems to emerge in the story, stop reading and help the client make a rice cake feeling face to represent the feeling. Give the client plenty of time to create a new face! At the end of the story, the client should have four or five rice cake faces completed. Afterwards, process which features in each face show how that face is feeling. This focus on physical affect as it is related to internal emotions can then be applied to the client's own life.

Processing Questions:

What feelings did you make into faces?
Which ones were the hardest to depict and why?
What part of each face shows the feeling? (The mouth shows happy with a smile. The eyes show sad with tears.)
How can you tell when other people are feeling these feelings...are there other parts of their bodies that show you?
What are some ways that being able to see people's feelings on their faces might be helpful to you?

Homework Assignment:

Pick one feeling this week and be a detective. Watch how different people show the emotion that you picked. For example, if you are being a detective trying to find out how different people show anger, you might notice that your mom clenches her teeth, your friend balls his fists, your little brother stomps his feet.   Be prepared to report on the different expressions during the next session.

Special Considerations:

Children with eating disorders may not be appropriate clients to use this technique with because it is a food-based intervention.   Children with serious social impairments may have a difficult time generating faces...because they are not good at noticing physical cues in the first place.   For these clients, the therapist will have to be more directive.   The homework assignment for these children may need to be as simple as "Look one person directly in the face today...make eye contact...and see if you can figure out how he or she is feeling."

Applications and Modifications:

This technique is meant to help children identify feelings based on physical cues.   Reading body language is one of the most important skills a child can learn in order to be successful. The feelings used to make the faces can come from stories that relate to the child's clinical issues or from the child's own life. This technique can easily be adapted for a group or family setting.   In this case, though, you might have each participant generate one feeling face and have the group create their own story.   The therapist begins the story and each person adds on, changing the story in some way that reflects the feeling face created by that group member.   The feeling faces can also be used to describe a whole series of feelings experienced by a single client.   This application can be particularly useful in processing grief and loss with child clients.

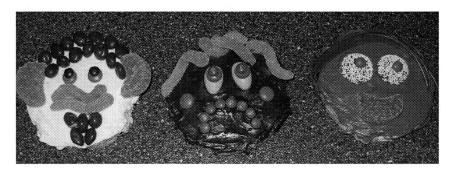

Mood Music

Treatment Modality: Individual/Group
Population: Ages 3 to adult
Treatment Phase: Working

Treatment Goals:

1. To bypass resistance to feelings verbalization by pairing a feeling with a non-verbal sound
2. To help the client identify appropriate feeling states that might result from antecedent events
3. To help the client recognize and work with various intensities or degrees of the same emotion

Props:

guitar
stories (fairy tales) (<u>Therapeutic Stories that Teach and Heal</u> by Nancy Davis can be used)

Procedure:

Begin by explaining that music is full of feelings and that many emotions can be communicated in music without ever saying a word. Compile samples of a wide range of music and play the samples for the client. Have the client label the primary emotion that she hears as she listens to each piece. Next, show the client a guitar. Real musical instruments are very special to children, and the privilege of getting to touch one will go a long way in getting the client to comply with the directions for the game. Instruct the client to listen carefully. Pluck each of the guitar strings, talking about how each string sounds different. Each emotes a different feeling. Let the client choose which note goes with which feeling (but be sure that happy, sad, mad and scared are included). Write the feeling words on small pieces of paper (or Post-it notes) and attach the appropriate paper to each guitar string. The client then gets to hold the guitar as the therapist tells a story. Tell the story, stopping abruptly at different points. The client will have to respond quickly (as with the game Musical Chairs) by plucking the string that seems to most closely mirror the feelings that the characters in the story might be experiencing at that moment.

Even the children who have the hardest time verbalizing their own emotions are surprisingly accurate in attaching the correct sounds (plucking the correct feeling strings) to various parts of the story. After the client has finished plucking strings (identifying feelings) for characters the first time, increase the difficulty of the exercise. Read the story again, This time the client must pluck the string gently if the character is merely irritated, or loudly if the character appears to be very angry. Through this process, the client is indirectly learning about modulation of affect and varying intensities of emotions.

Processing Questions:
Could you hear different feelings through the guitar?
Which string sounded the most happy? The most sad?
Do you think that all children pick the same feeling words for the same strings? Why or why not?
How did you decide which string to pluck at different times in the story?

Did most characters end up having several strings (emotions) plucked during the story?

Homework Assignment:

As you listen to stories in your classroom this week, try to guess how the different characters might be feeling at different points in the story. Also, try to find a piece of music that really seems to sound like how you feel most of the time and bring it in for us to listen to during the next session.

Special Considerations:

The youngest children might have difficulty remembering which feeling is attached to each string. Making picture cards (a happy face, sad face, etc.) and attaching these to the strings might help very young clients (or clients with learning disabilities) remember the pairing with greater accuracy.

Applications and Modifications:

This technique is a good starter activity to use with children who don't seem to want to talk at all and/or who seem threatened by direct questions or activities in which they are required to label their own feelings. The client is using a sound to represent a feeling (which is one level of removal) while trying to accurately judge the feelings of characters in a story (a second level of removal). The more removed the exercise is from the client's particular situation, the less resistance is encountered.

This game can easily be adapted to a group work format. Each time that the therapist stops abruptly after two or three sentences the client who has the guitar has to pluck a string immediately (as soon as the therapist stops speaking) that mirrors the events in the story. If she can do it quickly, she gets another turn. If not, the guitar is given to the next person. This musical chair-like quality to the storytelling encourages the client to pay close attention, making this a good practice activity for attentionally challenged children.

Another easy modification that may yield much projective information for the therapist is to have the client make up the story as she goes along. The only parameters are that there should be a beginning, a middle and an end to the story and the characters must experience each of the emotions labeled on the guitar at some point in the client's story.

Fruit Loops Feelings Necklace

Treatment Modality: Individual/Group/Family
Population: Ages 3 to adult
Treatment Phase: Working/Termination phase

Treatment Goals:

1. To identify feelings
2. To verbalize feelings
3. To practice appropriate feelings expression
3. To connect situations and actions to feelings

Props:

Fruit Loops™
twine
LifeSavers™
scissors

Procedure:

This technique is a modification of an idea created by a graduate student of mine, Marie Poss. Most children know and love Fruit Loops™ brand cereal. In this activity, Fruit Loops™ are sorted by color and the colors are used to represent different feelings. Begin the activity by sorting the Fruit Loops™ by color. While this is happening, talk about different feelings and how people can have all kinds of different feelings at the same time. Moreover, one particular feeling can be directed at many different situations or people at the same time. Give the client a piece of twine and a single Lifesaver™. Help the client tie the Lifesaver™ onto one end of the twine as a stopper (so that other LifeSavers™ and Fruit Loops™ won't fall off as they are added to the necklace). Instruct the client to pick one color of Fruit Loop™ (and the feeling with which it has been paired). For each Fruit Loop™ of this color that the child adds, she must make one feelings statement: "I feel _____ when _____". After several Fruit Loops™ of the same color have been added (at least five feelings statements have been made), the child gets to choose a Lifesaver™ of the same color and add it to the chain. This marks the end of one set of feelings statements. As the child adds the LifeSaver™ that will serve as a marker, ask the child to review all of her feeling statements and repeat the one that makes her the most angry. This process is repeated until all Fruit Loop™ colors have been used. At the end of the activity, the client is allowed to eat the chain.

Processing Questions:
What feelings did you talk about while making your necklace?
Which color do you have the most of on your necklace?
Which color do you have the least of on your necklace?
What parts of your necklace (i.e. which feelings statements) would you be willing to share verbally with someone else (a parent, teacher, friend)?

Homework Assignment:
Share one feeling statement from each color of Fruit Loop with a caregiver. Ask your caregiver to give an example of a time that he or she had this same feeling. (This allows the child to do field research and normalizes feelings for the child. Of course, the therapist must be sure that the caregivers will model appropriate feelings expression before involving them in the client's homework assignment.)

Special Considerations:
Children with eating disorders may not be appropriate clients with whom to use this technique because it is a food-based intervention.

Applications and Modifications:

This technique can *be* done individually with children, in a group setting or in a family session. The colors of Fruit Loops represent different colors and children decide the quantity of each color that is added to their necklaces. Therefore, a wealth of information can *be* gained regarding children's perception of their own feelings and how in touch they are with those feelings. The exercise can also help target areas for future work.

The technique can *be* adapted to reflect the grieving process. In this case, the client is encouraged to look at the series of feelings that have surface through the process of grieving. For example, the child was shocked first and then sad and then angry or vice versa. The Fruit Loops™ that represent each feeling would *be* added in that order.

The technique can also *be* used during the termination phase of therapy. In this case, each color would represent a feeling the client experienced during the course of treatment.

Example of a completed Fruit Loops Feeling Necklace.

Mood Manicure

Treatment Modality: Individual/Group
Population: Ages 5 to adult, but great for adolescent girls
Treatment Phase: Working

Treatment Goals:

1.   To identify and verbally express a range of feelings.
2.   To obtain the client's self-perception of the intensity of certain feelings
3.   To help the client make connections between situations or actions and feelings

Props:

several different shades of nail polish (red, pink, blue, green, black, silver, etc.)
vinyl cloth to protect furniture

Procedure:

Begin by helping clients attach a particular feeling state to each color of nail polish present. In a group setting, each client is given one container of nail polish. Each client will be responsible for painting anyone else's nails, if they ask for the color held by that client. Instruct group members that they must paint all their nails, but they may choose how many or how few colors to use. Everyone then helps to paint everyone else's nails. After all the nails are done, each group member takes a turn sharing her nails with the group, attaching an event or situation to each feeling represented on each nail. So, the sharing time might sound like this: "Well, the first three nails are red, because I get angry a lot. (Now she must name one event for each nail.) "I get angry when my mother doesn't listen to me. I get angry when people laugh at me. I get angry when I can't do my math problems right." The rest of the group listens attentively until everyone has had a turn.

Most teenage girls care a lot about beauty and fashion (I'm not making an argument for the healthiness of this, but it is culturally accurate.) This activity ends up feeling like a slumber party to the girls, and intimacies are shared and feelings universalized before they "know what hit 'em". Another aspect of this technique is that the girls end up physically nurturing each other. In order to paint each other's nails, they must pay careful attention to each other's bodies (hands) and they must touch each other (often holding hands in a sense) in order to apply the polish properly. Each group member has an opportunity to give and receive nurturing touch without even realizing it's happening. At the same time, the girls engage in the verbalization of feelings as well as antecedent events attached to those feelings.

Processing Questions:

How many different colors did you put on your nails? What feelings did these represent?

Were you surprised at any of the feelings/situations shared by the other girls?

Did any of the feelings/situations shared by others remind you of an event in your own life?

How did it feel to have someone else pamper you, by touching and painting your nails?

How did it feel to take care of someone else by touching and painting her nails?

What are some other quick and easy ways to pamper yourself?

Homework Assignment:

If someone asks about your multi-colored nails, share with them one of the feelings represented on your nails. Also, find one way to pamper yourself this week (use lotion on your hands, take a bubble bath, use chapstick to keep your lips healthy, etc.) and report back on it next week.

Special Considerations:

Children who have been abused or neglected may be uncomfortable with physical touch of any kind...or the level of attention given to them by peers in this activity. However, I would encourage them to participate, perhaps by asking them if there is one person in the group that they feel most safe with...and have that person do their nails. If absolutely necessary, a client can paint her own nails, or simply watch and listen to the others giving safe touches and verbal sharing in the group. Often children will be much more comfortable giving nurturing touch than receiving it. This issue should be fully explored and processed in the group.

Applications and Modifications:

This technique has been adapted for groups, but was first used to engage an eight year old (who thought she was fifteen) in the therapy process. She thought it was "childish" to talk about feelings and rolled her eyes at many of my interventions. As I wracked my brain, I thought that nail polish might be an appropriate stimulus for someone so invested in being a teenager. It worked like a charm. We were able to deepen the nurturing aspects of the therapeutic relationship (as I painted her nails and she painted mine) while she talked at great length about various feelings. It is important to have at least ten different colors of polish, so that if a child wants to explore a different feeling for each fingernail, she can.

This technique can also be adapted to explore the grieving process with clients. The stages of grief delineated by

Elizabeth Kubler-Ross lend themselves to this kind of activity. Have the client paint nails for whatever feeling they experienced first in their grieving process, second, etc. and then have her process the events, situations and timelines related to her loss. A client might end up with an explanation like the following: "The first two fingernails are painted silver, because when my mom died I just felt numb, frozen. The next two are red, because when I began to realize that she had been drinking and driving I was really mad at her." Etc, etc, etc.

Having lots of different colors of nail polish available will encourage the client to explore and verbalize a wide variety of feelings.

All Tangled Up

(a.k.a. The Worry Web)

Treatment Modality: Individual/Group/Family

Population: Ages 4 to adult

Treatment Phase: Working phase

Treatment Goals:

1. To identify and verbalize feelings of anxiety or worry
2. To externalize these worries or fears in order to deal with them concretely
3. To empower the client to take control of the anxiety and worry
4. To decrease the frequency, intensity and number of worries experienced by the client

Props:

a ball of yarn
scissors
paper
markers
finger puppets of bugs

Procedure:

This technique was developed for a four year old who came into my office "with a lot of worries". When I asked her to tell me what they were, she said "they're all tangled up". I brought out a ball of yarn and we used this to create the therapeutic metaphor for the session. Begin by telling the client "Everyone has worries and sometimes we have so many worries that they get all tangled up inside. It's hard to tell one from the other anymore. We just go around feeling worried and anxious without even knowing why. Today we are going to untangle those worries., Let's start by pulling out one thread at a time and naming it." The therapist then gives an example of one big worry and one small worry. For example, the therapist might say, "I get a little worried when we're out of milk, but I know we can go to the store and get some more." Then pull some yarn out from the tangled ball. Deliberately pull more yarn than is needed to represent this worry (perhaps three feet). Then say, "I worry this much about it" and hold up the length of yarn. Then say, "Actually, I don't worry quite that much about the milk, so I'm only going to make it this long" and shorten the piece of yarn by a foot. Help the client to untangle at least five or six worries. Some will be small and some may seem like miles of yarn. As the child cuts each piece of yarn (the length reflecting the intensity of the worry), write the worry in magic marker on a small piece of paper and tape it on the yarn (this helps delineate one worry thread from another). Then tell the client that you are going to tie the worries up all around the room until they look like a spider web. Tie one end of the yarn to the door handle and the other to the top of a bookshelf. Let the client choose where some of the yarn lengths get tied. However, they should criss cross each other across the space so that the threads end up looking like a spider web. When I did this technique with my four year old client, I invited the parent in to look at the web. It really helped the parent to understand the intensity of her daughter's worries to see them displayed three dimensionally. If a parent is invited into the session to witness the web, have the client verbalize each of the worries out loud. Then talk about ways to cut the worries down, so that the client will not continue to get caught in their web. Strategies for dealing with anxiety are then discussed. As the client verbalizes each strategy, she uses the scissors to cut down one thread of the web, until the web has disappeared.

Processing Questions:
Did you realize that you had that many worries inside of you?
What was happening in your feelings and behavior because of all these worries?
What are some of the things that you can do now to deal with the worries?
How did it feel to cut them down?

Homework Assignment:
During the coming week, when an old worry pops back up in your head, bring back the picture of cutting it down here in the playroom. Then use one of the strategies that we talked about to relax or divert yourself.

Special Considerations:
This technique may be overwhelming for young children if it is done all in one session. It can be divided up over several sessions by cutting and labeling the pieces of yarn one week, stringing them up into the web the next week, and cutting them down the next week. Some children may not want their caregivers to see their worries so clearly depicted. Honor the clients desires but try to uncover the underlying issue. Is the child ashamed to have so many worries? Has the parent ridiculed the child for worrying? Help the client work toward sharing the worries with a caregiver eventually.

Applications and Modifications:

This technique is easily adaptable to the group work format. Begin by having each group member generate one worry with which they struggle. Have each member cut a length of yarn that seems to represent the intensity of the worry. Use a large spider hand puppet and let each group member get a turn to pretend to be the spider as she strings her piece of yarn across the room and verbalizes her worry to the group. After all the worries are strung up and the web is completed, give each client a finger puppet of an insect (examples include smaller spiders, ladybugs, butterflies, bumblebees, etc.). Each group member must pretend that her insect puppet gets tangled in the worry web and "lands" on one string of the web. The only way that the insect can free itself from the web is to come up with a strategy to fight the particular worry represented by the string that it lands on. This allows the client who generated the worry to hear outside input on how to help it go away, while allowing each group member to participate in problem solving activities.

Although the web is usually strung all across the room, the picture shows the worries of an actual client, as well as the props that are used in the activity "All Tangled Up".

The "You Don't Scare Me" Spider Toss

Treatment Modality: Individual/Group/Family
Population: Ages 3 to adult
Treatment Phase: Working

Treatment Goals:

1. To verbally identify feelings of fear or anxiety
2. To identify specific fears or anxieties
3. To implement anxiety reduction tools through relaxation training
4. To increase the client's mastery of fears and anxiety

Props:
inflatable plastic spider and rings

Procedure:
This is a fun activity that motivates children to verbally express their fears and anxieties while taking positive steps to take control of them. Begin by talking about things that are scary to us. Tell the client,

"Lots of people are scared of spiders, so we're going to let the spider play the part of our fears. The goal of the game is to get the rings to land on the spider's legs. We will take turns tossing the ring. Each time that you toss the ring you must make one feelings statement about something that scares or worries you. "I feel afraid when...", or "I get scared when...", or "I worry about...". We will take turns tossing the rings until we have each gotten one on the spider's leg (and earned a token). Then we will go back over our fears and practice statements or techniques that help you feel less afraid or anxious. For example, if your fear is "I'm afraid that mommy and daddy will die while they're at work.", the client could practice saying to herself "Mommy and daddy are safe and I will see them tonight."

If a client says she is afraid of the dark, she can practice telling the darkness every night "You can't hurt me. I'm safe and my parents are right next door." Each participant gets to practice his counter-thought for the anxiety or fear he previously described and then toss another ring. A third round can be included. In this round, clients practice specific relaxation techniques in addition to the counter-statements they learned during the last round. This could be as simple as taking a deep breath, or as complicated as distracting themselves with a tongue twister. Each client practices the relaxation technique on his turn. If the rest of the group agrees that the client has done an adequate job of relaxing, this client gets another try at the ring toss. At the end of the game, tokens are traded in for prizes.

Processing Questions:

What happens in your body when you feel afraid?
What is your biggest fear?
What can you say to yourself to fight the fear?
Is there anything else you can do to relax and let go of the fear?
What are some times and places where fighting the fear might help you?

41

Homework Assignment:

Practice saying your counter-thought for one fear three times each day. Practice the relaxation technique that helps you fight the fear one time each day. Be prepared to report on how these exercises have affected your fear.

Special Considerations:

Although this technique may be good for groups because it universalizes "fear" as a normal feeling for children, some clients may have fears so intense or scary that they will not utter them in front of other people. In these cases, you can try playing the spider toss game one on one during an individual session or the client can just watch and listen to his peers. Also, children have a tendency to laugh at people when they show fear. The therapist must have a consequence ready for this eventuality. If a client laughs at another client's disclosure of fear, the first client loses a turn. Children love to do the ring toss, so the game acts as a built in motivator to keep children from this kind of negative peer pressure.

Applications and Modifications:

The technique can be adapted to use with groups of sexual abuse survivors., In these cases, the spider serves as a metaphor for the "creepy crawly" things that happened to them (see another technique, "The Creep and the Creepy Crawly). In the first round, clients share one creepy crawly thing that happened to them. In the second round, the clients pretend to make a statement to the perpetrator that places the blame squarely on that perpetrator. In the third round, the clients practice a self-soothing statement or strategy to use when memories of the abuse threaten to overwhelm them.

This technique can also be used in family sessions, particularly if the family is facing a situation together that is likely to engender a lot of fear or anxiety. Examples include moving, dealing with a chronic illness in the family, surviving a natural disaster or a car accident, etc.

42

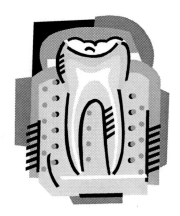

Fillings For Feelings

Treatment Modality: Individual/Group/Family
Population: Ages 5 to adult
Treatment Phase: Working

Treatment Goals:
1. To decrease denial in regards to painful feelings
2. To metaphorically associate secrecy with poor mental health
3. To identify and verbally express difficult feelings
4. To connect feelings with antecedent thoughts and events

Props:
several colors of clay including pink or red
digging and shaping tools
set of display teeth, like dentists use (optional)
page or poster of feeling words

Procedure:
Begin by asking if the client has ever gone to the dentist. Hopefully, the answer is yes. Ask if the client has ever had to get a filling. Explain that fillings are used after "stuff that hurts our teeth" has been left there for a long time, unseen, unbrushed and undealt with. This "bad stuff" starts to fester and turns into decay. Explain that the only way to make sure

our teeth stay healthy is to dig out the bad stuff and fill in the empty hole that is left. Explain that a similar process can happen with our feelings. Tell the client,

"If we get hurt by someone or something, but we don't look at it, the wound just festers, and ends up causing decay. In the same way that cavities start to hurt, our hearts start to hurt and we may not even know why. The only way to feel better then is to dig up the hurtful things and talk about them. As we share our feelings, the holes get filled back up with healthy feelings and a growing awareness. This means fewer trips to the dentist and to the feelings doctor."

Begin by making two gums out of red clay. Then make teeth sized balls or squares out of white or gray clay. Attach teeth to gums. The client is instructed to talk about an event in her life that has been hurtful to her in some way. As the client is naming the event, she is digging out part of the tooth. The client then describes the feelings associated with this event and fills the tooth back up with another color of clay. (The client should have already paired colors of clay with feeling words). The final product will be a set of teeth made out of clay. Each tooth will be filled with a colorful feelings filling. The client is encouraged to take this home and keep it. Children love to play with clay and the tactile work involved in the activity often gives clients greater freedom to speak about their pain. Their kinesthetic attention is focused elsewhere and allows their words to flow more freely.

Processing Questions:

What was your worst cavity (the event that you had spent the least time talking about or dealing with)?

What feelings did you realize you have about this event when you started to look at it?

How many different feelings ended up being represented in your fillings? Name them.

How does this activity apply to the hurts that happen in your life from now on?

44

Homework Assignment:

The next time that something hurts your feelings, even a little bit, find a safe person with whom you can talk about it. If there is no one available to you at the moment it happens, write it down and try to share it verbally with a safe person before the day is over.

Special Considerations:

Children who have had a very bad experience with a dentist may be put off by this activity. It would defeat the purpose of the exercise if the client ended up associating sharing his feelings with pain. However, most children will enjoy getting to be the dentist (the one with the power) and pretending to drill someone else's teeth.

Applications and Modifications:

The metaphor of removing decay after it has done unseen damage and then filling up the empty holes with something new and safe can have many applications. The technique can be used with children who are grieving the loss of a caregiver. In this case, the decay would be the unshared feelings of anger, sadness and fear that may be keeping a child stuck in one stage of the grieving process. After the therapist helps the client dig out these feelings and examine them, the holes can be filled back up with loving memories of the dead parent.

Clients who are diagnosed with Oppositional Defiant Disorder, Intermittent Explosive Disorder or Bipolar Disorder in Childhood can be helped to look at and talk about the events that lead up to their angry explosions. These clients can then fill up the holes with anger reduction strategies. Groups can create one set of teeth all together, or each member can create his own set of teeth, based on a common theme: anger management, self-esteem, grief and loss, etc.

Fillings For Feelings
(an example)

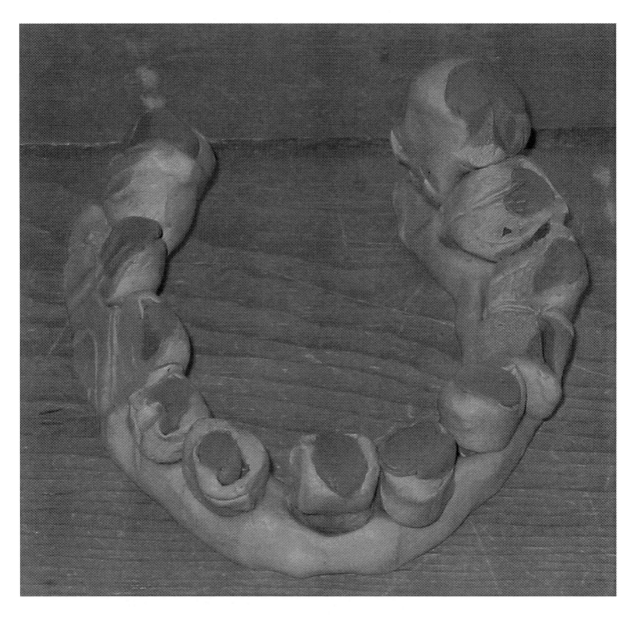

This set of "Fillings for Feelings" was completed by a ten year old female. Her feeling statements and the fillings that she made focused on one particular feeling. Having lots of different colors of clay available will encourage clients to discuss lots of different feelings.

Postcards In Motion

Treatment Modality: Individual/Group/Family
Population: Ages 6 to adult
Treatment Phase: Beginning/Working/Termination

Treatment Goals:

1. To communicate feelings through use of an expressive therapy technique
2. To help the client engage all of her senses in experiencing an awareness of self
3. To create a safe place to use in relaxation work

Props:

half sheets of construction paper formatted to look like postcards
markers, crayons, colored pencils, paints

Procedure:

(Step 1)   Lead the clients through a guided imagery with the following directions.   "Remember a place where you felt safe." (Different feeling words can be substituted each week, but it is best to help clients learn the steps of the exercise with "safe" as the stimulus.)   (Step 2)   Invite the clients to explore the place in their minds.   Ask questions that will help clients focus on the colors, shapes, sights, sounds, and smells of their safe place.   (Step 3)   Ease the clients out of the visualization and ask them to "write a   postcard from your safe place."   It is important to have prepared postcards available, as they provide a clean, projective, yet concise space in which to write. (Step 4) After clients have completed the text, have them turn the postcard over and draw an image of their place on the front of the postcard. There are no rules, although they may ask for some. (Step 5) Direct clients to put their postcards aside. Have them visualize their place again. Give them a piece of paper and ask them to write the numbers 1 through 4. Then ask them to pull out four words or phrases of the following types from their safe place: 1) an architectural element, 2) a small detail, 3) a main element (the thing that sticks out the most to them), 4) the mood or feeling of the place. (Step 6) After clients have generated their lists, ask them to come up with four body gestures, one to represent each of the four things that have been listed (you can liken it to charades). (Step 7) The next step is to have them decide in what order they want to string their gestures together. Have them practice doing the gestures in that order. In the group setting, clients can partner up and practice with each other. (Step 8) Finally, have the clients do the movement sequence while the postcard is being read out loud. The client may want to videotape their "postcard in motion" being performed. This is encouraged.

Processing Questions:

Was it difficult to visualize a safe place?
What was your safe place like?
How did the writing, drawing or gestures change your understanding of your safe place?
When are some times in your life when it would be helpful to go to your safe place?

Homework Assignment:

Every night this week, before going to sleep, close your eyes, imagine your safe place, and spend a little time there.

Special Considerations:

Some clients will have no memories of safe places. These clients should be encouraged to imagine a place where they could feel safe. Younger children can dictate the postcard to the therapist. However, they can complete the drawing and the gesture portions of the activity themselves. Some clients may feel embarrassed about using their bodies to make gestures in front of others. Take note of which expressive arts mediums are the most uncomfortable for her and use this information to guide future treatment planning.

Applications and Modifications:

This technique can be used in group or individual settings. The client can create a series of postcards over five or six sessions. The series could include postcards of a safe place, a scary place, an angry place, a lonely place, etc. This is an excellent activity for identifying and exploring a number of different feelings.

When this technique is used in groups, it can be adapted in many different ways. The whole group can participate in the guided imagery and relaxation component together and then create their own Postcards in Motion. Each participant can then perform her Postcard for the rest of the group.

The technique can be used as an assessment tool and new postcards can be generated at various points in therapy to assess the client's therapeutic gains. The technique can be empowering to victims of trauma, in that they are completely in control of how deep they want to go with the work. Moreover, this technique gets at psychological material through several different mediums and can function as a form of desensitization training with survivors of trauma.

This technique can also be used for time-limited groups. An entire 6 to 8 week anger management group could be constructed using the postcards in motion as the main intervention. Each session could involve the creation of a postcard *based* on a place where the client felt angry. Processing of the postcard could include increasing awareness of their physiological and psychological anger triggers, commonality across situations, irrational beliefs that show up, etc. The postcards are helpful in building a feelings vocabulary for children.

Lastly, families can benefit from this intervention. In session, the family can choose an event or an outing in which everyone participated. Each family member can then generate his or her own Postcard in Motion about this place and share it with the rest of the family. This kind of family activity helps members focus on the "good times".

The front picture of one child's postcard.

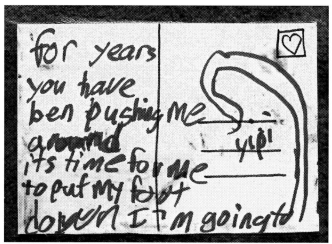

The flipside of the postcard shows the text portion of this child's postcard.

What Would You Be?

Treatment Modality: Individual/Group
Population: Ages 4 to adult
Treatment Phase: Working

Treatment Goals:

1.   To recognize and express feelings related to the divorce
2.   To normalize these feelings for the client
3.   To work with the feelings by assigning a concrete object to them
4.   To encourage the client's appropriate expression of her feelings directly to the parents

Props:

I Don't Want to Talk About It by Jeanie Franz Ransom
paper
markers
clay
Playdoh

Procedure:

This technique centers around a wonderful new *bibliotherapy* material called I Don't Want to Talk About It. It is a book about the emotional reactions of a young girl to the news that her parents are getting divorced. In each page she becomes a different animal with a different feeling. When she feels sad she becomes a fish so that her parents won't see her tears. At another point in the story she becomes a porcupine because she doesn't want anyone to touch her. The book does a nice job of giving children permission to feel any way at all about the divorce while connecting the feelings to behaviors. When I am working with a client whose parents are divorced, I read the client the story. At the end of the story, I ask the client what kind of animal they would like to be at this point in their parents' divorce. The client can show me by drawing or painting a picture of the animal, or creating the animal out of clay or PlayDoh. When the client has completed the project, I usually have him tell me why he chose that animal. I have him describe some characteristics of that animal. I may also have him make up a story about that animal. Two examples from my own practice follow: A four year old boy uses almost a whole body of green glitter glue to create a gigantic alligator so that he can gobble up his parents. A ten year old boy doesn't draw anything on his piece of paper. When I ask him about it, he says that he wouldn't be an animal, he would be an invisible man...so no one would bother him.

Processing Questions:

Which animal in the story did you like the best? Why?
What animal did you choose to be during your own parents' divorce and why?
Tell me some things that this animal does and feels.
Pretend to be the animal. What would it say to your parents?
What kind of animal would you like to be one year from now?

Homework Assignment:

Remember the words that the animal wanted to say to your parents? Pretend in your head that you are saying them to your parents and imagine their reactions. Also, take a few minutes each day to picture the animal in your head. Then picture yourself taking care of it...petting it, feeding it, playing with it. (The internal practice of saying the animal's words to the parents is in preparation for the child to eventually say these things to the parents. This second activity is encouraging self-nurturing)

Special Considerations:

Unfortunately, parents are at all different levels of wholeness and most parents who are going through a divorce are dealing with their own pain and may need a lot of extra support to be able to nurture their children well through this time. It is very healing for the child if you can get them to take ownership of the animal's words and speak them to the parent himself. However, I suggest that these be done in session (so that the child has you there as a support) and that the parent be briefed ahead of time on how to respond. If you do not believe that the parent can respond therapeutically, another option is to find a puppet that is the same animal as the one the child created. Have the child use the animal puppet and say the words to other puppets who represent the parents. The therapist can play the voices of the parents and convey therapeutic messages relevant to the child's issues.

Applications and Modifications:

If you are working with a divorce adjustment group for young people, this technique would be an excellent addition to the curriculum. Each participant creates her own animal, story and statements that she wants to say to or ask the parents. All the other group members listen as each describes her animal and her statements. This can be extremely healing for these clients as they realize that other people have the same thoughts and feelings and questions (even though some of these are angry or scary).

This technique could also be used during the termination phase of work with a client who has been seen for divorce adjustment issues. The client can do a series of pictures or sculptures that show the different animals that she was and feelings that she had at different points in her adjustment to the divorce. The animals can *be* compiled into a *book* or a menagerie that she takes home with her.

The alligator (above) is the drawing of a four year old boy who wanted to become an alligator during his parents' divorce so that he could destroy everything. This child was originally referred for anger issues having to do with destructiveness.

Self-Esteem

Bird Calls

Treatment Modality: Individual/Group/Family
Population: Ages 3 to adult
Treatment Phase: Working

Treatment Goals:

1. To increase self-awareness
2. To increase self-esteem by highlighting the client's sense of uniqueness
3. To create a positive self-talk message or a life message
4. To empower the client by encouraging her to define her own "voice"

Props:

stuffed birds of different varieties, each has a voice box sewn in that plays the bird song unique to that bird

Procedure:

I first ran across these remarkable birds at a bird store in North Carolina (before they were popular). As I picked up each uniquely colored bird and listened to its special bird song, I decided that these could serve as an excellent metaphor for the unique voice that belongs to each of our clients. Many of our clients have lost their voices due to abuse or life circumstances. Others never knew they had a voice to lose. Our job as therapists is in large part to help clients find their voices again. Eight of these little birds sit on the window sill in my office. When a child comes into the office and seems interested in the birds, I invite him to pull them off the window sill. We listen as he presses each voice box and listens to the songs of the different birds. Then we listen again, and try to attach words to the song...by looking at the bird's appearance and listening to the quality of the bird call. Some birdsongs sound happy, others sad or angry or lonely. The loon has a particularly sad, haunting song that seems to resonate with my child clients. One bird sings "CAAA, CAAA, CAAA" over and over again. The child might decide that the bird is singing "stop, stop, stop" or "please, please, please". The message that the child assigns to each bird gives the therapist information about what is going on in different aspects of the child's personality. If the child assigns a negative message to a birdsong, such as "I hate myself, I hate myself" or "Shut up, Shut up!" the therapist should take note of which bird is singing that song, but should not try to redirect the client until all the birds have been given voices. Then the therapist says, "You may not know it yet, but you have a song inside of you...a voice...that is just your own. Nobody else in the whole world can say it just like you. I want you to think up your own song (or chant, or mantra, or life song...whatever word they understand the best) and I want it to start with the words "I am". After the child has completed this statement, the therapist may invite the child to draw a picture of what kind of bird the child would be if the child were a bird. Then have him write his life song somewhere on the picture. If the therapist has time in this session, or in the next, she may decide to revisit the birds whose songs sent negative messages. The therapist might say, "You know, I've been thinking about that red bird (the one whose song goes "I hate myself, I hate myself"). I think it is a very beautiful bird and I feel sad thinking of how bad the bird must feel, singing this message over and over. Could you help me come up with a different message that the bird could sing to replace that one?

Processing Questions:

What characteristics helped you tell the birds apart? Were any two exactly the same?

Which one sang your favorite birdsong? How come this was your favorite?

Could you sense how different birds were feeling from their different songs?

What is your special song?

Homework Assignment:

Practice singing or saying your special song three times a day and be aware of how this singing impacts your feelings. Pick a person whom you really admire (a parent, teacher, actor, singer, friend) and try to figure out what his or her life song might be.

Special Considerations:

Children who are high functioning in the verbal arena are the best candidates for this technique. However, I have used the technique with an adolescent who refused to talk to me at all. I finally asked her to the birdsongs and choose the one that seemed to reflect how she was feeling just then. Although she didn't choose one, she said "None of them sound as sad as I feel." This became a jumping off point for the rest of the session.

Applications and Modifications:

This technique can be easily modified to fit a group format. Each group member is given one bird and asked to press the voice box while everyone else listens. Then each member comes up with words to accompany the birdsong of their chosen bird. Afterwards, each group member shares their creation with the group. The third phase would be asking each group member to create her own "life song" and share it with the group. In the group setting, the therapist can still ask each client to draw himself as a bird. The artwork can all *be* cut out and the birds can *be* hung from the ceiling.

This technique will work nicely with families too. The main focus of this technique when used with families is to explore how each member's voice adds to the uniqueness of the family unit...and to send the message that the family wouldn't *be* the same without all the voices.

Above is the whole set as they perch on the windowsill of the office, inviting clients to use them. Below is a close up view of the birds used in this activity.

The "Good-At" Game

Treatment Modality: Individual/Group/Family
Population: Ages 3 to adult
Treatment Phase: Beginning/Working/Termination

Treatment Goals:

1. To practice making positive self talk statements
2. To increase the client's sense of competence/mastery of the environment.
3. To increase overall self-esteem.

Props:

a can of Play-Doh™ for each participant
treasures (glass stones, coins, colored baubles)

Procedure:

Open a can of Play-Doh™ for each participant. Begin by telling the client, Instruct the client to take one little chunk of Playdoh and put it to the side. Roll the rest into a ball. Then press both thumbs into the middle (to begin to hollow out a center) and mold it into a shape that looks like a cup or a nest. Then take the leftover Play-Doh™ (that which was put aside) and place it in front of the client. Instruct the client to roll it into a ball and then flatten it into the shape of a pancake. Invite the client to create facial features for the flat circle of

Play-Doh™ using stones, coins, etc. from the treasure chest. When the face is finished, have the client fill up the rest of the Play-Doh™ (shaped like a cup or nest) with treasures. Put the lid/face on top of the cupped piece, covering up the treasures. The client has now created a rough Play-Doh™ person. The therapist points out that the Play-Doh™ person doesn't look very interesting from the outside. Since you can't tell a lot about this person from the outside, she has to be opened up. She has to tell us about all the things that make her special. Model pulling out one treasure at a time from the Play-Doh™ person's body while making a statement that begins with "I am good at...". The therapist should model statements like "I am good at laughing", "I am good at dressing myself", "I am good at listening." It is important that client begin to realize that skills and abilities that she may take for granted are part of what make her unique and special. The child then has a turn to make a "Good-At" Statement for each of the treasures in his/her Play-Doh™ person.

Processing Questions:

What could you tell about the Play-Doh person from the outside?
What was inside the Playdoh person and how is that like the things inside you?
Was it hard to think of things that you're good at?
How did it feel to say nice things about yourself?

Homework Assignment:

Ask three different safe adults (this could include the therapist, teachers, parents, clergy, etc.) to tell you one thing that they think you are good at. Be prepared to give the list to the therapist next session. The number of people that the children should consult may change depending on how many, or how few, positive influences the child has in her environment.

Special Considerations:

I have not yet found a client who didn't enjoy some version of this game. However, clients may have such low self-esteem that they can't think of anything they are good at. If this is the case, the therapist must voice true positive statements about the clients until the clients begin to believe them. Moreover, clients with *severe* speech delays or cognitive deficits may need modifications (*see below*).

Applications and Modifications:

This technique is particularly useful in a group setting *because* children who cannot think of many (or any) things that they are good at, can have their positive qualities reflected by other group members. This allows other members to feel important at the same time that the client *becomes* aware that not only is she "good at" many things, but other people notice and appreciate her skills and abilities. For children suffering from speech delays the therapist can invite the client to draw pictures for many different skills (or cut them out of magazines). Young clients can choose from the pictures and store the ones that match their abilities in their Play-Doh people. These pictures can then be produced when it is their turn to share their "Good At" statements.

This technique can be adapted to almost any population and setting. Often, when I give workshops, I give all the participants an opportunity to experience the technique. However, we use Smarties as the prop and for every Smarties, you have to say one thing that you are "Good At". Workshop participants often give feedback regarding how awkward it feels to say nice things about themselves. They report that it feels like bragging and that they can't think of many things that they are good at. If adults have this much difficulty with highlighting their positive qualities, how much more difficult it must be for children.

The "I Can" Mobile

Treatment Modality: Individual/Group/Family
Population: Ages 3 to adults
Treatment Phase: Working

Treatment Goals:

1. To enhance self-esteem
2. To increase awareness of self by using "I" statements
3. To assist the client to recognize and verbalize his competencies
4. To celebrate the client's skills and abilities
5. To create a concrete reminder of the client's competencies.

Props:

empty, washed soda cans
blank paper/ construction paper
tinfoil/sequins/feathers (other craft supplies)
markers/crayons
string

Procedure:

More than one session may be needed to complete this activity. Begin by helping the client generate a list of skills he possesses and, behaviors that he can complete with a successful outcome. Children (and adults) often have great difficulty appreciating their own abilities. Give categories of behaviors and examples. Examples include, "You take care of your body, you brush your teeth, put on your shoes, wash your face." Another category is how children relate to others. Tell the client, "You can smile at me, you can give hugs and kisses, you can say you're sorry, etc." Another category includes more traditional skills and abilities. Tell the client, "You can draw circles, you can count to ten, you can hop and skip." After the client has generated a list (ten to fifteen items), help the client choose five or six competencies. Art materials are made available, and the client creates some representation of the competency. This may be a picture of a child brushing his teeth, a pair of tennis shoes cut out of a magazine (for tying shoes), or an abstract symbol that has meaning to the client. The client then wraps each creation around an empty, clean soda can and attaches each can to the hanger with strings of various lengths. The client (or therapist, if the child is too young to write) writes the "I Can" statement that the picture represents on each can. When the mobile is complete, the client presents it to the therapist, group or family, by showing each can and saying "I can..." followed by the competency that is being highlighted on that can. Some examples are, "I can run fast,", "I can count to ten," and "I can share my toys."

Processing Questions:
Was it difficult to think of many things that you "can do"?
What makes it difficult?
How did it feel to verbalize all of your "I can" statements?
Where are you going to hang you mobile?
What will you think to yourself when you look at it?
What will you tell others who ask about your mobile?

Homework Assignment:
Each day for the next week, spend some time standing in front of your mobile, and repeating aloud your "I Can" statements.

Special Considerations:

All children can benefit from this activity because it enhances self-esteem. Children of various developmental levels will need different levels of interactions from the therapist. Very young children may need help generating the list and making the pictures or writing the "I Can" statements on the wrapped soda cans. Children with extremely low self-esteem may need to hear what competencies the therapist sees in them (over and over again) in order to complete the activity. The technique combines auditory, visual and kinesthetic learning, so all children should be able to participate on some level.

Applications and Modifications:

As this activity is a self-esteem builder, it is appropriate for many different problems and is beneficial to children with many different diagnoses. This technique can be done over the course of several sessions, using the first half of each session to work on a client specific issues like anger management, social skills, etc. The last half of the session can be used to create one 'I Can' can to add to the mobile.

This technique may be particularly suited to a group setting. If a client is unable to generate many of her own "I Can" statements, her peers can help her. For example, Sally may say, "You can do math problems really quickly.", or "Remember how you hit the ball the other day in P.E." The group setting also allows for a greater number of witnesses as the client verbalizes her competencies. As with all creative activities, the therapist will have to help group members create an atmosphere of appreciation for each other's mobiles while offsetting competition and comparison.

This technique can also be used in a family setting. Each family member can do his or her own mobile, or the family can create one mobile together. It could function as a family crest of competencies. An "I Can" mobile can also be made during the termination phase, as a way of helping the client recapitulate or review all the skills she has learned in therapy.

For example, a client's termination mobile might include statements like, "I can take deep breaths", "I can talk about my feelings", or "I can ask a friend to play".

The mobile featured above is an example of the kind of mobile that would be created by a very young child in that there are no words, only descriptive pictures of the things he can do.

Magnifying The "Feel Goods"

Treatment Modality: Individual/Group/Family
Population: Ages 6 to adult
Treatment Phase: Working

Treatment Goals:

1. To practice magnifying positive statements made by self and others
2. To practice minimizing negative statements made by self and others
3. To empower clients to control input from the environment
4. To increase self-esteem

Props:

a magnifying glass
paper
pens
whipped cream or shaving cream

Procedure:

Begin by talking with the client about the messages other people give us and the messages that we repeat over and over again to ourselves. These messages can help us to feel good about ourselves or they can make us feel bad. Explain that we cannot always keep people from saying ugly or mean things to us, but we can decide what we do with them. Take the can of whipped cream or shaving cream and ask the client to try to remember one mean thing someone has said to her, or that she has said to herself. Unfortunately, if the child is school aged, it won't take her long to remember something unkind that has been said to her recently. When she produces the statement, for example "You dress funny," write it out in big letters with the whipped cream. Point out how big it is and how much space this one "feel bad" message takes up. Then have the client come up with several messages that are "feel good" messages. Maybe they are statements her parents have made, or kudos from kind teachers. The therapist can contribute positive statements to the list also. Lastly, the child will write down the positive messages that she gives herself (be sure that some of the other self-esteem exercises from this book have been done first...so that the child already has an arsenal of positive self-talk statements). Give the child several very small pieces of paper. Have her write the "feel good" messages as small as she can...teeny tiny...so that they are very hard to read. Then give the child the magnifying glass and talk about how it is up to her to "accentuate the positives" or to magnify, by repeating over and over again, the "feel good" messages she receives while ignoring the "feel bad" messages. Have her use the magnifying glass to read, out loud, the teeny tiny "feel good" statements. Then have her look back at the large "feel bad" message that was written in whipped cream. It should have turned into liquid by now and be much smaller. Perhaps it has disappeared entirely. Tell the client, "While you were making the "feel goods" bigger, the feel bad message shrunk (or disappeared)."

Processing Questions:

Why do you think the "feel bad" messages seem so big to us?
Who in your life gives you "feel good" messages?
What can you do to remember and magnify the "feel goods"?

What will happen to the "feel bads" as you focus your attention on the "feel good" messages?

Homework Assignment:

Record at least one "feel good" message sent to you from a friend, teacher or parent each day this week. Write these messages in very, very tiny writing and bring them in next week. You will use the magnifying glass to read your list to the therapist.

Special Considerations:

Children who are not old enough to read will not be able to get the full therapeutic benefit of this technique. Parents and other caregivers can be powerful allies in getting this metaphor across, but the therapist must assess whether or not the caregivers are psychologically and emotionally able to show support to the child through consistent use of "feel good" messages before enlisting their help.

Applications and Modifications:

One nice variation of this technique is used in work with families. Explain to the parents this whole concept of magnifying the positives and encourage them to make a conscious effort to send more "feel good" messages to their child this week. Parents can "slip" teeny tiny "feel good" statements to the client during the week, that are then brought to therapy and read using the magnifying glass. The family can create an "accentuate the positive" board at home. That board should include plenty of the smallest size of blank, colorful Post-it notes, push pens, and a (plastic) magnifying glass that hangs from a piece of yarn on the board. Each family member is assigned another family member to whom she will write one teeny tiny "feel good" message each day. All messages will be posted on the board and each family member is required to use the magnifying glass once a day to magnify whatever message is addressed to her.

Caging The Mistake Snake

Treatment Modality: Individual/Group/Family
Population: Ages 3 to adult
Treatment Phase: Working

Treatment Goals:

1. To externalize negative self-talk
2. To control negative self-talk by setting limits on the externalized messages
3. To give the client an experience of mastery over negative statements

Props:

a finger puppet snake
a hand puppet snake
tiny plastic snakes
larger rubber snakes
stuffed snakes
clay
yarn

Procedure:

Young children have difficulty grasping the concept of self-talk. To "talk to yourself in your head" is an abstraction. If the therapist can get the child to externalize the messages...that is, to pretend that the source comes from another voice outside himself, he can more easily fight it. In this activity, the snake becomes the externalized messages and, consequently, the enemy. Begin *by* processing the kinds of statements that make us feel bad. Explain to the client, "We hear them in our heads, but we are going to begin to pretend that they come from outside ourselves." The child generates two or three negative messages with which she struggles. The client gets to pick a snake from all the various kinds of snakes mentioned above. Tell the client,

"I'm going to pretend to be the snake. Let's pretend that your teacher has asked you to draw a circle. The snake slithers up to your ear and hisses, "That's not a good smiley face. Sally's is better. You might as well stop trying."

Depending on the client's current level of self-esteem, the child might very well say "O.K." or "You're right" to the snake the first time. Process with the client how it made the client feel and how the client would like to handle the snake. Further explain,

"Now that you know it's coming, you can *be* ready and have a plan for making it be quiet. It can only talk to you if you let it."

Help the child come up with a strategy. Some clients may want to address the snake directly and say, "Be quiet, snake. You are a liar. I'm doing my best and that's good enough." Of course the length and complexity of the response will vary with the age of the child. What I prefer to do is help the child find some way of containing the snake, of gaining physical power over it. For this reason, it is important to have options available. Examples include a jail, a box, and a set of blocks. The child may even decide to bury it deep in the sand box or to have it swallowed by another puppet. Once the snake has been caged, this metaphor can *be* used with the child whenever he is struggling with another negative message.

Processing Questions:

What is the "feel bad" message that bothers you the most?
When is the snake most likely to come and whisper it in your ear?
Who is in charge of your response?
What can you say or do to the snake to make it go away?
What are some other times in your life when it would be helpful to cage the snake?

Homework Assignment:

Every night before you go to bed, practice talking back to the snake...you can do this out loud or in your head. You can also bring back the picture in your head of how we caged the snake in the playroom.

Special Considerations:

This technique would be contraindicated for children who suffer from any form of psychosis. For these children, the reality testing is so skewed that the pretend metaphor of the snake may be confused with hallucinated voices in their heads. Every time that this technique is used the child should be coached in the reality/pretend distinction.

Applications and Modifications:

Again, this technique can be easily modified for a group setting. In this case, each participant chooses a snake to represent the communicator of her most troublesome negative message. Each participant plays the voice of his own snake and all the other group members get to generate helpful responses to the snake and empowering ways to get rid of it. The child for whom the negative message exists will feel empowered to deal with the message while being given lots of options, in a supportive environment, for getting rid of it.

Caging The Mistake Snake
(an example)

Here the "Mistake Snake" has been locked in jail and can no longer hiss negative self-talk into the client's ear.

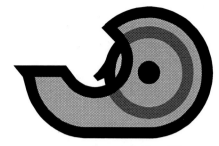

Repairing Self-Esteem

Treatment Modality: Individual/Group/Family
Population: Ages 5 to adult
Treatment Phase: Working

Treatment Goals:

1. To make the client aware of negative self-talk
2. To illustrate the damage that this negative self-talk causes to self-esteem
3. To generate replacement statements for the negative self-talk
4. To increase self-esteem

Props:

paper cutouts (they can have a gingerbread shape or look like real people)
miniature scotch tape dispensers (regular scotch tape dispensers can be substituted)
colored pens

Procedure:

Begin by asking the client if anyone ever says mean things about him, like "You're dumb", "You're fat", etc. Talk about how easy it is to start repeating the negative things we hear about ourselves from other people...and how quickly these negative thoughts become our own thoughts. Give the client a gingerbread cut out. Challenge the client to pretend that the gingerbread cut out is himself. Have the client write down the things that he thinks about himself that make him feel bad. Give examples like, "I'll write some on mine," "I can't do anything right," and "I have to make straight A's or I'm a loser." Be sure that each statement is written down on a different part of the cut out body. After he is finished, instruct the client to tear each body part off as you say the negative statement out loud. Process with the clients the ways in which negative self-talk "tears us apart". Once the client has ripped up his person, begin to talk about how self-esteem gets rebuilt. Have the client turn each body part over and write on the blank side a positive counter-thought for the negative self-talk statement represented on the other side of the body part. For example, the statement "everybody hates me" can be countered with "I have some friends" or "my parents take care of me". It is important to help the client create alternate statements that he/she can believe in. The client may need lots and lots of help from the therapist for this part of the activity. When the negative tapes are playing in our heads it is hard for us to think of alternative truths. Each time a counter-thought is created, it is written on the other side of the torn body part. When the client has all new positive self-talk statements, the positive side of each body part is taped back together. This serves as a metaphor for rebuilding the person's "I am", the person's self-esteem.

Processing Questions:

What are some of the things you say to yourself that make you feel bad?

What happens when you say these things to yourself over and over again?

Who is in control of your thoughts?

Can they be changed?

How does it feel to replace a "sad" thought with a thought that helps you feel "O.K."?

How can you build up your self-esteem?

Homework Assignment:

Make a copy of the positive person who has been taped back together. Tell the client to take this home and put it on his mirror. His homework is to say every positive self-statement on his taped up gingerbread person two times per day... when he gets up in the morning and when he goes to bed. If there is a supportive caregiver in the home, the caregiver can reinforce and witness the twice daily ritual.

Special Considerations:

Young children will have difficulty with this activity because it requires reading and writing. The therapist will have to play a more active role for these children. Children who have suffered abuse of any kind may have the negative self-talk so deeply ingrained that they cannot even generate positive alternatives. In this case, the therapist must do it for the client and then help the client to practice the new messages...over and over and over again.

Applications and Modifications:

The side of the gingerbread cutout that has been taped back together with the positive self-statements displayed can be photocopied over and over again. Send one home with the client (so that he can begin practicing the positive self-talk everyday). Inform that child that he is going to create a paper doll chain...by pinning up one copy of the positive self-talk doll this week and then stapling (taping, sewing) another exact replica to it next week. When the chain is long enough to go from one side of the client's bedroom door to the other, the client can take it home. Each week, in order for the client to add a replica to the paper doll chain, he must say each of the positive self-talk statements out loud while the therapist acts as a witness. Another interesting variation to this would be to leave the face of each copy blank and let the child fill in the facial expression each week after reading the positive self-talk statements aloud. In this way, the therapist may *be able to* use the dolls as an assessment measure, since the affect that the client draws on the paper doll's face is likely to mirror her own emotional state at the time of each visit

Both the group and family therapy settings can make appropriate use of this technique. An added benefit of doing this technique with several people is that more ideas are generated and each participant gets to hear positive things said about himself.

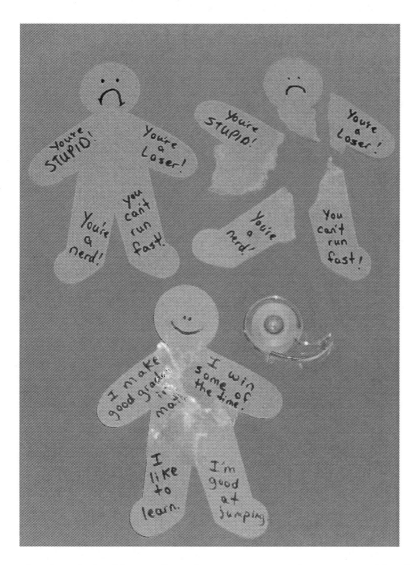

The top left side of the picture features the person with the negative self-talk statements written on it. The top right picture shows that same person after the client has said the negative self-talk statements out loud and torn them apart. The bottom portion features the person after the positive counter thoughts have been generated and the person has been taped back together.

Congealed Cognitions

Treatment Modality: Individual/Group/Family

Population: Ages 7 to adults

Treatment Phase: Working

Treatment Goals:

1. To identify irrational beliefs and automatic thoughts
2. To understand concretely that these are ingrained in our thought processes
3. To generate rational belief statements and positive self-talk
4. To practice thought replacement

Props:

red Jell-O™
whipped cream
a brain mold
paper/pens
plastic wrap

Procedure:

This technique will need to be done over several sessions. It may not take the whole of each of these sessions, however, so plan other activities or child centered play time. Begin by talking about our helpful brains and our unhelpful brains. Give examples of things that our brains do when they are being "unhelpful", like generating irrational beliefs and automatic thoughts. Examples should be generated that children can related to, such as "I never get good grades,", "I always mess up,", and "I should make 100% on all my assignments." Write some of these out on cut up pieces of paper. Have the client circle the words that make the statements irrational or impossible (words like all, always, never and should). Then help the client pick one area of her own life that is plagued by irrational beliefs...it might be schoolwork, it might be social relationships, it might be her own self-image. Have her write down four to five negative self-talk statements that play over and over again in her head. Talk about the way these thoughts become solidified or congealed in our minds. Wrap each piece of paper in plastic wrap or put each piece in an airtight baggy so that it will not get wet. Then make the Jell-O™/whipped cream recipe and pour it into the brain mold. Talk about the ways in which our minds can be molded or changed. Create word pictures of neurons firing in the brain and new connections being made. A peer makes the statement, "You stink!" to the client. If the client gives the statement play time in her mind, it plays over and over and she begins to believe, irrationally, that she really does stink. Have the client "implant" the negative belief statements wrapped in plastic wrap into the liquid that is in the mold. Put the mold in the refrigerator so that it can congeal before the next session. At the start of the next session, take the brain out of the refrigerator. See if the client remembers some of the negative self-talk statements that were put in the mold. Talk about the behaviors that these kinds of beliefs generate in people. Dig out the negative thoughts and unravel them (taking them out of the plastic wrap). Tell the client that the first step in replacing those unhelpful thoughts is knowing what they are. Now that the client has "dug them out" and "ruined" that old, unhelpful brain, a new, helpful brain will have to be built. Together, look at each negative self-statement and generate a rational, reasonable replacement thought. For example, if the unhelpful thought was

"I always have to make 100% on my papers to be a good student", this can be changed to "It feels good to make 100%, but I'm a good student every time I try my best." There are many other replacement thoughts that could be generated for this one example. Work with the client until she has come up with a statement that relieves her anxiety. Once you have all the replacement thoughts written, refill the Jell-O™ mold with clear Jell-O™ and try to arrange the new thoughts so that they can be read through the Jell-O™. (Make some kind of ritual out of throwing out, ripping up, or burning the old thoughts). Put it in the refrigerator to congeal. Next session bring it out and practice the new thoughts. If you want to, you can eat the Jell-O™ together to get the new thoughts (figuratively) inside of you.

Processing Questions:
What are the harshest negative things that you say to yourself about yourself?
How do you feel after you think these things?
Is there anything that you can do when you think unhelpful thoughts?
What are some of the positive things that you can say to yourself instead?
How do you feel after you think these things?
How did it feel to rip up the old thoughts?

Homework Assignment:
Practice hearing your own negative self-talk and stopping it. Once a day, write down a thought that you have that makes you feel bad about yourself. Then write down a counter-thought...one of the thought we put in your new brain. Say this second thought out loud three times and see how you feel.

Special Considerations:
Children must have some ability to self-monitor and understand their thought processes. Preschool age children will not be able

to glean as much from this technique as older children *because* they are not yet proficient at thinking about thinking.

Applications and Modifications:

In most problems of childhood, from low self-esteem to depression to oppositional behavior, to trauma, cognitive distortions play some role in the dysfunction. Therefore, the construction and practice of replacement thoughts as well as the fun of getting to play with Jell-O™ and brains makes "Congealed Cognitions" a wonderful activity for child clients.

Social
Skills

All The News That's Fit To Tell

Treatment Modality: Individual/Group

Population: Ages 3 to adult

Treatment Phase: Beginning/Working/Termination (this technique can become an opening ritual for every session)

Treatment Goals:
1. To identify and verbalize a feeling state.
2. To help the client make connections between situations or actions and feelings
3. To assist client in setting and verbalizing goals for treatment.
4. To increase positive self-talk.

Props:
microphone
poster

Procedure:
Begin by explaining that each person will get a turn to pretend to be a T.V. anchorman/woman or a talk show host. Each person will get a chance to interview someone else and to be interviewed. (I always tie appropriate completion of this activity to a token economy system.) The therapist goes first,

in order to model appropriate silly behavior. An example follows: In a news anchor kind of voice, "Good evening and welcome to Channel Five's News at Five. My name is Paris Goodyear-Brown and I'm here interviewing Johnny about his day." Then ask each of the following questions:

1. How are you feeling today?
2. What's happening that's helping you feel that way?
3. What's one goal that you're going to work on?
4. How are you going to work on that goal? (optional for younger children)
5. What's one thing you like about yourself?

These questions are written on a poster somewhere in the room as a reminder, but even young children quickly learn and remember the questions and can recite them. When a child is asked "How are you feeling today?" he will often respond with the words "Fine," "O.K.," or "Good." These are not feeling words and should not be accepted. In each group I run, the children will eventually start to call each other on it and mimic me by saying "Fine is not a feeling word. Try again."

Once all the questions have been asked and answered, the interviewer says "Thank you for sharing." The interviewee says, "Thank you for listening." Eye contact is also promoted throughout the game. Clients earn a token for appropriate completion of this feelings check-in.

Processing Questions:

How did it feel to be a celebrity, interviewing others?

How did it feel to be the interviewee, answering questions?

Was it easy or hard to think of one thing you like about yourself?

How did it feel to tell your peers one thing you like about yourself?

Was it hard work for you to make eye contact during the interview? If yes, what made it hard?

Homework Assignment:

Go home and interview one of your caregivers using these questions. If you do it often enough, it may *become* a part of your dinner conversation.

Special Considerations:

This technique requires verbal skills, so children with speech delays might have more difficulty. Also, younger children or children with cognitive delays might not remember the questions (or *be able to* read them from the poster). In this case, the therapist can give clients verbal prompts. It's also important to have some feel for the emotional states of the children as they enter group on any given day. If a client has had a family member die, for example, he will understandably need a long check-in, to process his feelings. When one client honestly shares something important like this with the group, it sparks the other clients to remember their own losses. It is almost like the floodgates open and everyone wants to share their grief. This can make for a powerful session, *but* it requires that the therapist *be* willing to sacrifice her agenda for the session.

Applications and Modifications:

This technique is a wonderful way to *begin group sessions*. I have used it with every children's group I've ever done, and if I forget to start with this feelings check-in on a given day, the children ask remind me. Each member wants to be the first to hold the microphone and the group members settle in to the group quickly in order to be first. It's also a fun way to start individual sessions with a child.

Depending on what kind of a group is being run, (a divorce group, an anger management group), a topic specific question can be added to the end of the feelings check-in. For instance, "What's one time that you controlled your anger this week?" If this becomes part of the weekly check-in for an anger management group, it naturally raises the accountability level for the members. They are more likely to look for opportunities to control their anger, because they will be required to report on it "on national television!"

This picture illustrates one kind of microphone that can be used. With clients who refuse to speak to therapist or other clients directly, the client can be directed to choose a puppet and be the voice of the puppet as the puppet is interviewed.

"I Feel" Hopscotch

Treatment Modality: Group/Family

Population: Ages 5 to adults

Treatment Phase: Working

Treatment Goals:

1. To identify and verbalize feelings
2. To practice "I feel" communication statements
3. To connect feelings with behaviors
4. To increase the client's skill with conflict resolution

Props:

sidewalk chalk
stories
sidewalk
(if you don't have access to a sidewalk, you can use rubber
floor mat puzzle pieces arranged like a hopscotch board
indoors)

Procedure:

Children love this technique because it is a variation of a
familiar childhood game. Begin by discussing the importance of
"I feel" statements as a conflict resolution strategy. Contrast

these statements with "You are" accusations and allow the children to talk about how each kind of communication makes them feel. Take the children and let them help draw a hopscotch board. Explain that this is a hopscotch board that will help us practice our "I Feel" statements. Within the boxes of the grid write the words "I Feel" and leave one blank..."When"...and leave one blank "Because" and leave the last one blank.

Different scenarios that describe conflict are then generated. Fairy tales, Aesop's Fables, bibliotherapy materials, or real situations that the children experience at school can be the used for the content. For example, a child describes being tripped in the hallway. The child hops through the boxes saying the words of the "I Feel" statement and filling in the blanks. "I feel angry when I am tripped because I could get hurt." Each child earns a token when they successfully complete the hopscotch board. Again, auditory, visual and kinesthetic learning are occurring, so the lesson is likely to have more staying power for the clients. Clients are likely to need lots of help in the beginning, because "I Feel" statements don't come naturally to most of us. It feels good to accuse others and say hurtful things when we are angry and it can be very difficult to stop and think before responding. Clients will often ask for this game again and again because it gives them a feeling of mastery...while giving them some outside play time.

Processing Questions:

How did it feel to make accusations?

What was it like to make "I feel" statements?

How do you react when others accuse you?

How did you feel as you listened to other group members make "I Feel" statements.

Can you think of some times in your school day when making "I Feel" statements can help you get along better with others?

Homework Assignment:

Make an "I Feel" statement once a day for the next week. Be prepared to talk about how people reacted to this form of communication.

Special Considerations:

The verbal format may be too complicated for very young children (3-5) to be able to internalize and repeat. These children might just do the first part "I feel mad" and then hop through the rest of the squares.

Applications and Modifications:

This technique is best suited for group, so that clients get an opportunity to practice the new skill themselves, but they also get to watch other peers come up with "I Feel" statements and be on the receiving end of these communications.

A family can play this game together as a way of addressing the "blame game" that often happens in families. Moreover, it's a good way to encourage the new communication patterns to be modeled for the client by the parents.

You Can't Mask It

Treatment Modality: Individual/Group/Family
Population: Ages 3 to adult
Treatment Phase: Working

Treatment Goals:
1. To help the client become aware of her own body language
2. To help the client correctly interpret the non-verbal cues of others
3. To learn self-modulation in response to the body language of others
4. To increase social skills

Props:
a wide variety of masks
a video camera or a full length mirror
tokens

Procedure:
Begin the activity by introducing the concept of body language. Children with social deficits tend to have a very hard time making eye contact and correctly interpreting the non-verbal cues of others. Explain to children that out of all the

communications that we send to each other, very little is comprised of the actual words we use. Another portion of communication is the tone and volume, but most of our communication is made up of what our bodies do while we interact with others. Talk first about the cues that you can get from people's faces (this is a good activity to do in conjunction with the Rice Cake Feeling Faces). This concept can be introduced by trying to communicate the feeling of boredom with body language. If the treatment modality is group, have the clients pair up. Instruct one to begin talking about her day. The therapist instructs the other to act interested for a minute and then to show boredom. After the first partner has picked up on the second partner's message and stopped talking, the partners switch roles. Afterwards, process the non-verbal cues that were used to communicate the message "I'm bored with what you're saying." The clients will probably list things like rolling eyeballs, covering the mouth, stretching, looking around the room, etc. Point out that the client never said a word, but effectively communicated a message. There are likely to be clients who are so unused to watching non-verbal cues that they missed the message and just continued talking and talking. Obviously, clients benefit from more practice. Explain to the clients that they are going to become detectives of non-verbal cues. The therapist challenges the clients that she's going to make it harder to detect the non-verbal message by putting on a mask. The therapist puts on a mask and then assumes a body posture. She then asks the clients to guess how she is feeling. After the correct feeling is guessed, clients share the non-verbal cues that tipped them off. Each client gets a turn to wear a mask and "perform" a body posture that communicates a certain feeling to the rest of the group. The non-verbal cues that were noticed are discussed after every round. Children earn a token every time they try to communicate a feeling while wearing the mask. The tokens are traded in for prizes in the end.

91

Processing Questions:

What did you have to do to pick up on non-verbal cues?
Did everyone use the same body language to show the same feelings? What were some of the differences?
What were the most common non-verbal cues for anger? For sadness? For excitement?
When are some times in your own life when reading body language could be helpful?
Do other people read *your* non-verbal cues correctly?

Homework Assignment:

Use your new detective skills at least once each day to figure out how a friend, teacher, or parent is feeling. Later, check out your conclusion with the person and see if you were correct. Be prepared to report on your detective work next session.

Special Considerations:

Children who suffer from symptoms included in the Autism spectrum (including Asperger's Syndrome) can benefit greatly from this activity. However, they may need much more help from the therapist.

The psychological pain and mistrust of others can be so intense in some clients that all they can see in others is a projection of their worst fears or their own anger. Therefore, these children may say that everyone looks angry or bored or "mean" even when the non-verbal cues point to another feeling. These clients need more work using trust building activities, processing their own anger, engaging in reality testing with the therapist and learning how to do take other people's perspective.

Applications and Modifications:

This technique is motivating for clients because they get to try on masks and "pretend". They feel successful when they accurately communicate or detect other clients' non-verbal cues during the game. When the other clients cannot guess the feeling, the client with the mask on is asked to face the full length mirror and change his body posture, until he believes he has enough non-verbal cues for the other group members to accurately guess the feeling message.

This technique can be a wonderful help in families because it helps everyone become more aware of the complexity of communication that happens in their home everyday...and how to read it. This technique can also be done one on one in session and the client and the therapist can take turns being the detective. In this case, it is helpful to videotape the client posturing the different feelings. Watch the tape with her later, processing how clear her non-verbal cues are.

 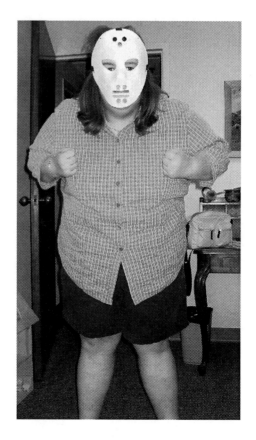

The client has to guess how the person wearing the mask is feeling, based solely on body language. On the left, the feeling being portrayed is sad. The feeling being portrayed on the right is angry.

The Twizzler Test

Treatment Modality: Individual/Group/Family
Population: Ages 5 to adult
Treatment Phase: Working

Treatment Goals:

1. To develop appropriate physical boundaries with others
2. To increase appropriate, positive social interactions with peers

Props:

Twizzlers™

Procedure:

Begin by talking about boundary issues with the client. Explain that sometimes we feel uncomfortable around people when they get in our physical space. In the same way, others may not like us as much if we get in their physical space. Many of our clients have great difficulty understanding and implementing appropriate physical boundaries. Some clients will hug complete strangers and sit in their laps, while others won't get close enough to a peer to work a puzzle together. Sometimes this boundary training is done using the concept or "arm's length". For example, if the client is talking to a good friend, a good rule of thumb is to have one arm's length of distance between them. In this activity, the Twizzlers™ (which are about 10 inches in length) replace the arms. This activity is great for group work. The therapist can give several Twizzlers™ to each group member, have them break into pairs and measure various distances between the two of them using the Twizzlers™ as measuring rods. Each set of partners should decide on how many Twizzlers™ they consider to be an appropriate physical distance between a) a parent and child, b) two friends, c) a child and teacher and d) a child and a stranger. All group members share their decisions and compare them, coming up with the best "rule of thumb" for each scenario. The final distances are laid out on the floor and everyone gets a chance to "feel the distances" by standing at either end of the Twizzlers™. Then have the clients role play getting in each others' space. One client will step one Twizzler™ length closer to the other client than what would normally be appropriate. The client who is having his personal space violated must practice setting a verbal boundary by letting the encroacher know that he is feeling uncomfortable and asking the encroacher to step back.

Processing Questions:
What is a physical boundary?
What makes them important?
How many Twizzler lengths is a good distance between you and a friend?
What can you say if someone gets closer than you want them to?

Homework Assignment:
Use these new boundaries with people at home and at school and see what happens. Be ready to report on how the physical distances seemed to affect people.

Special Considerations:

Clients who have been sexually abused may have very inappropriate touching boundaries. These clients will benefit from some individual training regarding appropriate touches before they engage in this activity with peers.

Applications and Modifications:

This technique is a fun way for children to understand the concept of physical distances and to apply this to boundary issues in relationships of varying kinds. It lends itself to implementation within a group setting, but could also be done with individual clients. Setting clear boundaries with others serves to empower young clients. Moreover, children who are ridiculed because of their lack of social grace may find more acceptance among their peers if they begin to honor other people's needs for physical space.

This technique could also serve as a jumping off point for talking about physical violence. Fist fighting, pushing, tripping, etc. are all ways of violating another person's physical boundaries and are therefore unacceptable.

The technique could be modified for use in family sessions. In the tradition of family sculpting, the Twizzlers could be used symbolically to show emotional, psychological or physical distances from other family members. Each family member could take a turn arranging the family with a certain number of Twizzlers connecting them. Processing this activity with the family may help to shake some of the dysfunctional boundary lines and create newer, healthier ones.

Building Blocks of Communication

Treatment Modality: Group/Family

Population: Ages 3 to adult

Treatment Phase: Working

Treatment Goals:
1. To increase compliance with adult requests
2. To build cooperation
3. To increase effective communication skills
4. To give the client an experience of overcoming frustration and completing a task

Props:
two identical sets of blocks

Procedure:
This is a wonderful parent training tool. Begin by having a parent and one child sit on the floor with their backs to each other. Each is given an identical set of blocks. The number and design (color and shape) of the blocks can vary depending on the age and functioning level of the client system. For example, if a child is only three, give them each three blocks.

For young children who know their colors, using colored blocks can be helpful. However, if your client is a ten year old, you may use six blocks per person and make sure that they are plain wood. This increases the difficulty level.

The parent is instructed to build something. Then the parent is instructed to help her child build the same exact structure, but they are not allowed to look at each other's blocks until the task is completed. Therefore, the task becomes one of communicating clear, succinct, verbal instructions and waiting until the child has understood and completed that step before giving the next direction. Parents comment over and over again about how eye-opening this technique is in helping them understand that the words they use are not always understood by their children. When a parent says, "Take the large rectangle and turn it sideways...", this could mean three different things to the child. Parents end up learning to check in with the child about her perceptions and her understanding of the direction before going on.

This is an excellent activity for parents of ADD children, who need training in how to break down directions into a step by step process and how to ensure follow through of one step before going on to the next. I often make the comparison to asking a child to clean her room. The parent says "Clean your room" and the child begins to pick up the clothes and then gets distracted by the Lego's and forgets to finish. The parent must accompany the ADD child to the room and go area by area, saying "Please put the books back on the shelf." Wait until that task is accomplished and then say , "Great job! Now lets put the socks in the drawer."

After the parent helps the child through the activity, the child gets a turn to "be the boss", create a structure and give directions to the parent on how to build it. This usually becomes comical because young children are egocentric and believe that their parents can see whatever they can see. They leave out many descriptors and the parent usually gets lost. The therapist can assist the child in coming up with clear directions if necessary. Sometimes the process takes a long time and either the parent or the child or both get frustrated. It is important that the therapist encourage them to finish. At the end of the activity, both participants see that they created exactly the same structure by working together and it gives them an incredible sense of mastery and unity.

Processing Questions:

What was the hardest part about giving directions?
Did your words always have the same meaning for you and your partner? How so?
What did you learn to do differently to get the other person to understand you?
How does this new learning apply to your parenting?

Homework Assignment:

Practice giving one direction and wait until it is completed before giving the next one. Do this at least once a day and be prepared to report on the results next session.

Special Considerations:

A client with very a low frustration tolerance or an extremely short attention span will find this activity torturous. The goals of increasing the attention span and extending the client's tolerance for frustration must be met before this technique is introduced. Parents who are abusive and unable to use helpful language with the child should obviously be excluded.

Applications and Modifications:

Although this technique is well suited to parent training, it can be used in individual sessions with the following goals: to help the client increase attention, follow directions quickly, and communicate effectively. I have also used the technique in a group setting with 10 year old boys. In this adaptation, two group members are chosen to sit back to back. The other group members watch the two in the middle try to communicate effectively to build the same structure. If the partners get stuck, they can ask the watching group members for help. The group members can phrase a direction for the leader to repeat to the builder. The watching group members are not allowed to blurt out hints. If the partners in the middle turn around to look at each other's work, they get replaced. The whole group can process issues related to communication and cooperation at the end of the exercise.

The clients sit back to back, like the puppets pictured above. It is against the rules to look at what the other person is building. Only verbal communication can be used to make sure that both people end up with the same exact structure. Although plain wood blocks are preferable for older clients, blocks with colors and shapes (pictured below) are helpful in giving directions that younger children can understand.

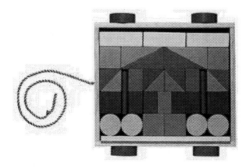

Marshmallow Walls

Treatment Modality: Individual/Group/Family

Population: Ages 3 to adult

Treatment Phase: Working/Termination

Treatment Goals:

1. To tear down a dysfunctional pattern
2. To replace a dysfunctional pattern with functional behavior
3. To promote healthy boundaries in relationships

Props:

marshmallows
peanut butter
plastic butter knife
markers (or gel icing pens)

Procedure:

The last time that I used this technique was with a ten year old boy who was having a major problem with arguing. He is very, very smart and can argue at great length with adults and peers alike. However, it does not help him to build positive relationships. I asked him to make a list of phrases that he uses to keep arguments going. This is the list he generated: "No", "That's not quite right.", "Actually", "Uh-uh", "Not really", etc. He wrote each of these phrases on different marshmallow.

At my direction, he built a wall using peanut butter as the mortar between marshmallows. A little figure was chosen to represent him and this figure was put him behind the wall of marshmallows. We discussed how his arguing builds a wall between him and his friend and parents. We decided to knock that wall down and build a new wall of "Giving in Gracefully" statements. These statements included: "I see your point", "Let's agree to disagree", "O.K.", "You might be right", etc. The client practiced saying these phrases as he wrote them on new marshmallows. His first wall had been tall, so that no one could see around it, keeping him in social isolation. The second wall was more like a fence and after it was put together, it still served as a boundary around him, but it was a long, low wall. Metaphorically, he was then able to see and communicate with others. Of course, the most fun part is getting to eat the leftover marshmallows and peanut butter at the end of the session.

Processing Questions:
What were some of the thoughts and phrases on your first wall?
How did these affect your feelings and behavior?
How did it feel to knock down the wall that kept you from others?
What thoughts or phrases did you use to build your second wall?
How will these affect your feelings and behavior?
How can you apply this to your life?

Homework Assignment:
Choose one phrase from your second wall each day and say it over and over again to yourself...or in conversation with others. Notice how this affects your relationships.

Special Considerations:
Children with eating disorders may not be appropriate clients to use this technique with because it is a food-based intervention.

Applications and Modifications:
This technique can be used as a metaphor for any kind of a wall that children build around themselves. It may be a wall of negative self-talk: "I'm fat, I'm stupid, I'm worthless". It may be a wall of shyness: "I don't know what to say, What if they laugh at me", or it might be a wall of worries, "What if mom gets killed in a car wreck?, What if the school burns down?, What if I have cancer?" It is simply a matter of understanding what is troubling the child, characterizing the problem as a wall that has been built around the child, working to tear that wall down and rebuild a new, more functional wall.

This technique is a wonderful one to use for boundary work. Children who run up to strangers, touch people inappropriately and over-disclose may end up reflecting this in a first wall that is really just a jumble of unattached marshmallows signifying extremely loose boundaries. As the dysfunctional thoughts are challenged and new, healthy boundaries created, this can be reflected in a new wall that serves as a healthy boundary between the child and others. This focus on boundaries also makes it a useful technique to use in work with families.

In a group setting, the therapist can choose a topic: anger management, self-esteem, etc. Each group member can generate a dysfunctional thought/phrase that contributes to the problem. All group members help to put the wall together and knock it down. Then all group members help generate the new, healthy wall.

Marshmallow Walls
(an example)

The wall pictured above is the problem wall. Each marshmallow represents an irrational thought, negative self-talk statement, unhelpful behavioral response, negative coping strategy, etc. In this example, the wall is made up of phrases that a 10 year old male client uses to keep arguments going. The wall below is the new wall. Each of the statements above was evaluated and an opposite response was generated and written on the new wall. Notice in the picture below that the first wall has been knocked over and shown to be no longer functional for the client.

Fishing For Compliments

Treatment Modality: Group

Population: Ages 3 to adult

Treatment Phase: Working

Treatment Goals:
1. To enhance social skills
2. To increase the client's ability to make positive verbalizations to others
3. To enhance self-esteem

Props:
tinfoil or shiny wrapping paper
Swedish Fish™ candies
Gummy Worm™ candies
paper clips
labels

Procedure:
The shiny paper (representing a fish pond) is put in the middle of the group. A label is placed in each of the four corners. The labels represent different categories of compliments. A Swedish Fish™ (each of a different color that corresponds to the label) is placed beside the label. The labels might read as follows:

"Physical attributes"-examples of this kind of compliment include "You have pretty hair. I like your smile."

"Skills and Abilities" -examples of this kind of compliment include "I like the way you dance" or "You're very good at reading."

"Self -Care (Keeping Yourself Safe)" -examples include "I like the way you look both ways before you cross the street" or "You bring very healthy snacks to school."

"The Way You Treat Others (Social skills)" examples include "I like the way you usually say please and thank you." or "You're good at playing with everybody"

Place enough fish of each color in the middle to allow each player to "catch" one fish of each color (if there are 3 players, there should be 3 red fish, 3 green fish, etc. in the middle). Each player is given a gummy worm and a paperclip. Unfold the paperclip and stick one end through the Gummy Worm™, which will act as the "bait". Each player takes a turn "catching" a fish. They must give a compliment to someone in the group that comes from the category that corresponds the color of the fish they have "caught". The game is over when all players have caught a fish of each color. They will then have practiced making four different kinds of positive statements to others.

Processing Questions:
How did it feel to receive a compliment?
How did it feel to give one?
Which category of compliment do you give most often?
What are some situations where giving a compliment might be a good idea?

Homework Assignment:
Give one compliment to three different people each day and write down their response.

Special Considerations:

People suffering from eating disorders or other food related issues (allergies, health concerns) may *be* better served with a magnetized fishing game.

Applications and Modifications:

This technique is great for use in groups of children diagnosed with ADD, ODD, CD, *because* most of these children lack social skills. This technique is also great for family therapy, in that it gets the family members making positive statements to each other. Lastly, magnetized fishing poles and plastic fish can *be* found at discount stores...if the use of food is contraindicated.

This is an example of the board for "Fishing for Compliments". The player is dangling a Gummy Worm over the fish, trying to decide which kind of compliment to give.

Attraction and Repulsion

Treatment Modality: Individual/Group
Population: Ages 4 to adult
Treatment Phase: Working

Treatment Goals:

1. To recognize and increase behaviors that attract other people
2. To recognize and decrease anti-social behaviors
3. To practice social skills
4. To increase the frequency of positive peer interactions

Props:

a large horseshoe shaped magnet
several smaller magnets (or)
a Geo-Mag™ building set

Procedure:

Begin by talking to the client about the forces involved in magnets...how two magnets can result in a strong attraction and attachment, or a strong repulsion, so that they push each other away. Explain that the client has the same power that the magnet has... he can draw people to him or push them away through his behavior. The therapist buries several magnets in the sandtray...under a very thin layer of sand. The client is given the big magnet. When the client finds a small magnet that is pulled toward the large magnet, he has to verbalize one way that he can attract other people to himself. If she finds a magnet that is repulsed by the big magnet, he has to describe one way that he can push people away. Keep two running lists, one of behaviors that attract peers and the other of behaviors that repel peers. After this game has been played once, the lists are reviewed. Process with the client which of these behaviors she is already "good at" and which behaviors need more practice. The clients that we see often suffer from some social deficits and have difficulty maintaining positive peer relationships. In the second round, deliberately arranges all the magnets so that they are repulsed by the large magnet. Challenge the client to see if he can change a repulsion to an attraction. The client has to role play or practice one pro-social behavior and if he does it convincingly (or has a puppet do it convincingly) then he gets to turn over one of the repelling magnets, so that it is immediately pulled toward the big magnet.

Processing Questions:

Did all the magnets have the ability to attract and repulse each other?
How is this like yourself?
What were some of the attractive behaviors you came up with?
What were some of the repulsive behaviors that you came up with?
Which behaviors are you going to practice?

Homework Assignment:

Pick one of the attractive behaviors that you identified and practiced in the game. Practice it two times a day and see how other people are affected by the behavior. Be prepared to report on your findings next session.

Special Considerations:

Children who have severe social deficits may have no idea how to attract others to themselves. The therapist will take a much more active role in throwing out alternative behaviors to these clients. These clients will need practice, practice and more practice.

Applications and Modifications:

This same technique can be used in group, with each participant taking turns hunting for a small magnet with the large magnet and then describing a pro-social or an anti-social behavior. One nice aspect of doing the activity in a group setting is that clients can partner up and role play the pro-social behaviors in front of the group.

Another fabulous prop that I recently came across is a product called Geo Mag™. It includes lots of stick shaped plastic coated pieces and each end of each piece is magnetic. Each set also includes several metal balls. Incredible shapes and structures can be built out of the materials if the clients can get the right ends to attract at the right time. This product may be better suited for groups because there are so many pieces. It promotes cooperation among group members.

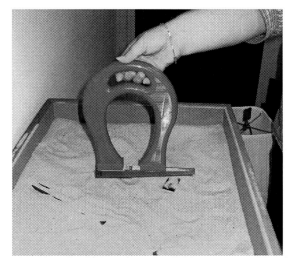

In the above picture, the player has unburied a magnet by attracting it (pulling it out of the sand) with the larger magnet. The client must now verbalize one behavior that he can use to attract others to himself.

Anger Management

Anger Buttons

Treatment Modality: Individual/Group/Family
Population: Ages 5 to adult
Treatment Phase: Working

Treatment Goals:
1. To identify anger triggers
2. To make clients aware of physiological responses to anger
3. To connect feelings with behaviors
4. To begin taking ownership for how anger is handled

Props:
gingerbread people cutouts (in paper or felt)
buttons of varyings shapes and sizes
glue/yarn
markers

Procedure:
This technique is useful in helping clients become more aware of the situations or actions that "set them off". I prefer to talk about "anger buttons" as opposed to anger "triggers" in part because the latter has connotations related to guns and may be sending questionable messages to children. To introduce the technique, begin by talking about things that make us angry. Ask the question, "Do you ever feel like you are not in control of your anger? Someone says something and before you know

it, you are making an angry response. I call that an anger button. Sometimes I feel like I have different buttons all over me, and all someone has to do is press that button and I blow up. Does that ever happen to you? Help the client to generate examples from her own life. "Some things make me really angry, and other things just irritate me." Model choosing buttons of different shapes and sizes to reflect varying degrees of anger. Each client is given a cutout of a person (this will represent him/herself) and asked to arrange her anger buttons on the cutout. The placement of buttons may correspond to the body parts in which the client holds her anger. For example, Sally might place the anger button that represents "someone making noise during a test" over her mouth, because it irritates her and makes her clench her teeth. She might put another anger button (someone laughs at me) over her hands, because this usually results in her hitting someone.

After the anger buttons are attached, which can be done with glue or (if felt cutouts have been used) with yarn, the therapist can begin a discussion of who presses these buttons. The button metaphor is an excellent way of helping children see that they are giving their power away if they "allow their buttons to be pressed". This technique also increases clients' awareness of the connection between feelings and behaviors. This can be a great jumping off activity for other anger management/reduction skill building.

Processing Questions:

What are your biggest anger buttons?
How do you usually respond when someone presses them?
What are some of the buttons that just irritate you?
How do you usually respond when someone presses it?
Do you think most people know your anger buttons, or are they hard to see?
How can you change your responses to people when they try to press your anger buttons?

113

Homework Assignment:

(1)"Hide" one of your anger buttons one time today and see what happens. (2)Watch a friend today and see if you can figure out one of her anger buttons.

Special Considerations:

Children who can't yet write will need help with that piece of the exercise. Also, watch young children carefully (small parts are involved and you don't want a child to swallow a button). A certain subset of children may be in extreme denial about anger issues. These clients are often perfectionistic, care taking children...or children who have learned that it is not O.K. to be angry in their family. They may need special assistance to examine their anger buttons.

Applications and Modifications:

This technique is adaptable to individual, group and family sessions. In the family setting, it is interesting to have the whole family contribute to the creation of each family member's anger button cutout. It is interesting to see who knows about how to get at other family members and who is oblivious to anger buttons in others. The patterns of anger in the family (generational issues) can also be assessed through this activity. This technique may be particularly useful to clients who have a hard time taking responsibility for their own feelings and actions. The child who gets into fights everyday and always says that her peer "pushed her to it" is a an example of this phenomenon. This child will enjoy getting to enumerate her anger buttons, but may begin to have a paradigm shift when the therapist talks about "letting others press your buttons" as a way of giving away power. This may be the first step in accepting responsibility for the feeling of anger and the behaviors that result.

The therapist might consider using robot cutouts (instead of people), particularly for boys, because they generally love technological stuff and may understand the "button" metaphor more easily when talking about a computer.

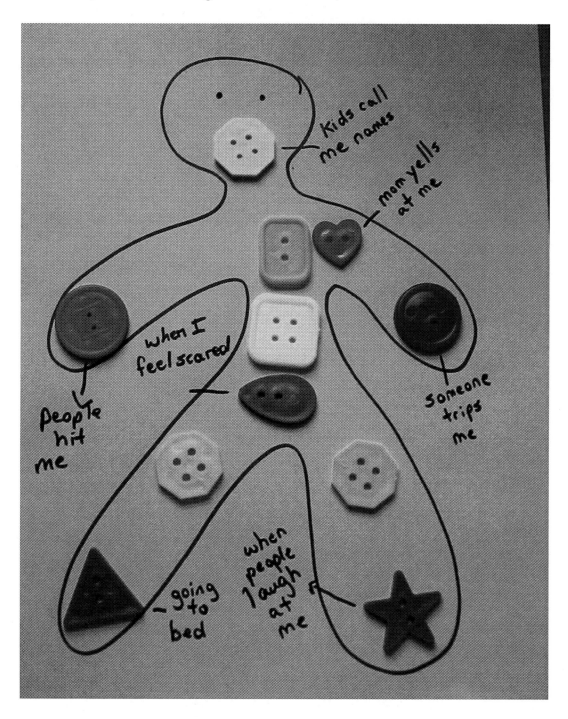

The above picture is an example of the completed "Anger Buttons" activity. Where the buttons are placed on the body can have behavioral significance for the child. For example, the "going to bed" button and the "when people laugh at me button" are on this person's feet. When this child becomes angry about either situation, his behavioral response may be to kick.

Blow It Up, Blow It Out!

Treatment Modality: Individual/Group/Family
Population: Ages 3 to adult
Treatment Phase: Working

Treatment Goals:

1. To become aware of various degrees of anger
2. To connect feelings and thoughts to actions and situations
3. To decrease the client's frequency and intensity of anger outbursts
4. To relieve the internal pressure created by holding angry feelings inside through catharsis

Props:

long skinny balloons
big cardboard thermometer

Procedure:

Begin by introducing the concept that anger can be experienced with various degrees of intensity. Show clients the thermometer and compare the rising temperature to anger rising up. Mark different places on the thermometer and attach stickers that give words for anger that reflect various intensities. For example, attach the word "irritated" or "annoyed" at 65 degrees Fahrenheit, the word "mad" or "angry" at 85 degrees Fahrenheit, and the word "enraged" or "furious" at 100 degrees Fahrenheit. Hold up one of the long skinny balloons next to the thermometer and explain that the clients will be blowing up the balloons to various degrees of anger, using it like a thermometer. Model the prompt that should be used in each round. "I get irritated when people cut me off in traffic." Blow up a balloon (be sure to put a little too much air in it). Hold up the balloon for everyone to see and then pretend to rethink it and let a little air out (making the length shrink). Then say, "Yeah, I get that much irritated when people cut me off in traffic." Each client gets a turn to make a statement that begins with "I get irritated when..." and to blow up their balloon a little bit. Everyone has two more rounds. The prompt for the second round is "I get angry when...," and the prompt for the third round is "I get furious when...". By the end of the third round, everyone should have their balloons blown up to their full length. Each client chooses one more thing that makes him angry and writes it on his balloon. Process what happened each time they made an anger statement and blew up the balloon. Ask the clients, "Where is all that anger now?" The clients usually answer "inside the balloon." Invite each group member to decide on how he is going to let his anger out. Most clients will choose to pop the balloon. The clients who choose this course should be encouraged to make their anger statements (the one written on the balloon) loudly and pop their balloons one at a time. The rest of the group members act as witnesses. Some clients may want to sit on their balloons or stomp on them until they pop. The occasional client will want to take his balloon home with him, put it on a shelf and let the anger seep out slowly. Often, the method by which the client decides to get rid of the anger inside the balloon is an accurate description of how that client handles anger in most situations.

Processing Questions:

Are you able to tell the difference between different levels of anger in your own life?

What does your body do when you are irritated? Angry? Furious?

What was it about some situations that made you angrier than others?

How did you choose to dispose of the anger? Is this how you usually handle anger?

Homework Assignment:

Keep a running list this week of the times when you get angry. Try to distinguish between different levels of anger. Use at least one unusual word for anger when describing your feelings to someone this week.

Special Considerations:

Young children may not be good at blowing up balloons yet. You may want to have a balloon pump available (I recently found one at the dollar store) for those children. Attention seeking or impulsive clients may try to make the balloons squeal or pop them "accidentally" before the appointed time. This can usually be avoided by firmly telling clients that they only get one balloon each and that they should treat it with care. The squealing can be handled by positively reinforcing the clients who keep their balloons quiet and letting them go first in each new round.

Applications and Modifications:

This technique lends itself well to a group setting, mainly because the clients have their experiences of anger normalized. Since each client ends up generating and verbally sharing four different anger statements, some antecedents are bound to overlap. It also helps the child to feel more powerful during the portion of the exercise in which they get rid of their anger if their are witnesses to the act.

This technique can *be used* in individual sessions. It can be adapted for use with victims of abuse, as they process different layers or levels of anger related to their perpetrator. In these cases, it is helpful to encourage the client to take the balloon home and let the anger seep out gradually *because this is more likely to mirror the real process for victims* (as opposed to setting up a metaphor that would pressure the survivor to let go of the anger all at once as would be done if the balloon was popped).

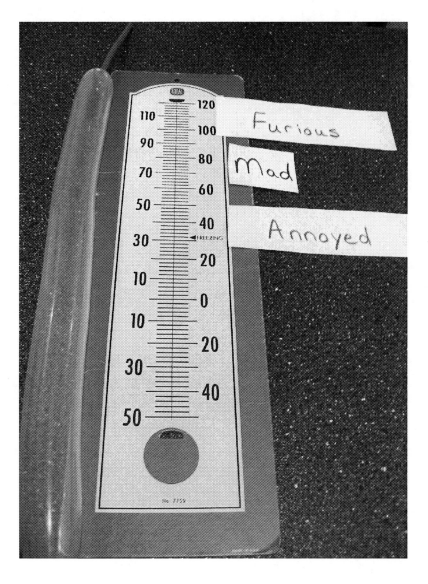

The above picture shows the cardboard thermometer that is used for this activity, as well as the words for various degrees of anger placed at various degrees along the thermometer. The balloon shown has been through three rounds of anger verbalizations, including the "I feel furious when..." statement.

"I'm Sick Of"...Eggs

Treatment Modality: Individual/Group
Population: Ages 3 to adult
Treatment Phase: Working

Treatment Goals:

1. To identify anger triggers
2. To verbalize anger while involving kinesthetic activity
3. To experience catharsis of anger

Props:

plastic sheeting
uncooked eggs in the shell
markers

Procedure:

This activity is a wonderful anger release exercise...and if done carefully, should result in an experience of catharsis in relation to the immediate anger stimulus for the client. I developed this technique when I was doing school-based counseling. It was the week of Standardized Testing and my clients (most of whom were also Learning Disordered) were strung tighter than a bow. This technique allowed them a release of frustration that "cleaned them out" and prepared them for the next day of testing. Explain to the client that we all have things that we get "sick of". Feeling "sick of" something can make us really angry. If we hold all this anger inside, it festers and affects our behavior, so we're going to practice getting it out. Warn the client about how delicate the uncooked eggs are, and that each client only gets one egg. (The desire to participate in the final activity usually keeps clients from cracking or breaking the egg too early). Each client is given an egg and a marker and has to write on the egg one thing that they are "sick of". Almost all of my clients said "I'm sick of sitting...or testing...or filling in tiny bubbles." Then each client gets a turn to throw her egg and smash it against the plastic sheeting, *while making the "I'm sick of" statement out loud.* This direction is given extra emphasis in the text *because it is* the verbalization combined with the kinesthetic action that allows for catharsis. An argument can *be* made that just smashing the egg could *be* positively reinforcing aggression. Process the activity with the client.

Processing Questions:
How did it feel to smash the egg?
How do you feel now?
Are there other times or situations where you can pretend to put your anger in an egg and smash it?
What are some other ways that you can safely let your anger out?

Homework Assignment:
The next time that you get angry, pretend to put that anger in an egg and visualize smashing it against the wall. Be prepared to talk about what happened to your anger and your behavior.

Special Considerations:
Children who are so impulsive that they won't be able to safely hold the egg (delay gratification) should not be given the egg until it is their turn to throw one. Also, it is important to draw a clear boundary between what can be experienced in the playroom (smashing an egg) and what can be done at home. We don't want our clients getting into trouble because of an idea we introduced!

Applications and Modifications:

This technique can be used in the individual and group setting. It can be modified for use in individual therapy to process angers related to an abuse situation. Children can process anger related to parents, teachers and peers. Anger related to the death of a family member or a chronic illness can be "put" in the egg and smashed. The main consideration regarding anger release work of any kind is maintaining firm boundaries about when and where it is allowed. You will not have served the child well if she goes home, smashes all of mom's eggs against the new couch and has serious consequences. The limits of the playroom and the "different kind of things that can be done in here" should be stressed again and again. This technique is a great jumping off point for other anger reduction techniques and can be used in a module on anger management.

Shake It Off

Treatment Modality: Individual/Group/Family

Population: Ages 5 to adult

Treatment Phase: Working

Treatment Goals:

1. To implement conflict resolution strategies
2. To empower clients to take control of their anger responses
3. To train clients to detect cues to escalating situations and avoid them
4. To decrease frequency and intensity of altercations with peers

Props:

gel-based sticky hands (different novelty stores carry them)

Procedure:

This technique is another product of finding a prop that has great potential and creating a therapeutic metaphor that kids will enjoy. Sticky Hands are hard jelly based products. The more common forms of the substance are sticky jelly balls with arms and legs. Play therapists often have children throw these against the wall to vent anger or to act out revenge on a perpetrator. The hands are similar, only the sticky jelly is shaped into an open hand with a long tail that looks like a long skinny arm to which the hand is attached. This technique is

123

meant to help clients recognize interactions with peers that may lead to conflict and equip them to withdraw from the conflict without "losing face". Begin by telling a story about a little boy who always got into trouble at school. "Everyday at school, someone would tease him, or say something to him to start a fight. The parents said to ignore him. The little boy tried this, but it didn't seem to work. Whenever he ignored the bullies, they just got louder. He didn't know what else to do. Introduce the idea of being "grabbed" by someone's words. When a peer says calls the client's mother fat or ugly, this is an attempt to grab the client and suck him into a conflict. Explain to the client, "Grabbing you is the bully's first goal and pulling you into an angry response is the second goal. It's easy to be grabbed. It only requires the bully saying something mean, but you don't have to get pulled in. If you respond, you are giving away your power and the bully is in charge. We're going to practice being grabbed by a bully's ugly words...and shaking them off, in order to avoid a fight." Then ask the client for some examples of statements peers make that usually pull her in. The therapist and client stand a foot or two apart. The therapist holds the long end of the sticky arm and throws the rest of it (much like a fishing pole), making the catch hold of the client and stick to her arm, shoulder, leg, etc. Make one of the "grabbing statements" while "casting" the Sticky Hand. Once it is attached to the client, the client has to make a verbal response that will de-escalate the situation, while helping her save face. (The client may need lots of help from the therapist in crafting the response.) Once the child can make the response verbally, in a way that is convincing, she gets to shake off the Sticky Hand. The client then gets a turn to "cast" the Sticky Hand onto the therapist and help the therapist come up with a "saving face" response.

Processing Questions:

What are the words that grab you and draw you into fights?

What do your peers want to happen when they say mean things to you?

What is the best way to break loose from their Sticky Hands?

What is required to break free when peers grab you with their mean words?

What are some other times in your life where shaking it off could be helpful?

Homework Assignment:

Take your sticky hand home and teach your parent or caregiver how to "shake it off" when someone grabs you with words. Practice shaking off anger one time per day. Be ready to report on how your response impacted the other person's behavior.

Special Considerations:

Very young children might have difficulty following through with the application of this technique, because it requires the construction and practice of various phrases (and the language may be too complex for them). Children do need more strategies for dealing with peers than just "ignoring". Although ignoring is a powerful tool, some children are just unable to do it consistently. The problem is even more complex for these children, because their difficulty in ignoring is often accompanied by a quick temper and impulsive responding. These children may need to practice "Stop and Think" skills or deep breathing exercises as part of the sticky hand technique in order to buy them time to come up with a response that will allow them to shake it off.

Applications and Modifications:

Very young children could benefit from a variation of this technique that does not require complex language. For these children, the sticky hand can serve as a warning that they are being "grabbed" by the mean words of a peer. However, the response training in this case is more behavioral. Very young clients can *be* trained to recognize the grabs and "shake it off" by physically *breaking* away from the situation and going to get a teacher's help. Again, this technique can *be* easily modified for a group setting. Each client gets a Sticky Hand and the therapist *breaks* clients up into partners. Each partner set makes up a situation in which a client is being "grabbed" by someone's ugly words. They also come up with a way out that "saves face". Each pair performs its role play for the rest of the group and the role plays are processed.

The Sticky Hands shown above are only one of several versions. This product can be found in various colors and sizes. They are also inexpensive, so that each client can take one home as a therapeutic reminder to "Shake It Off." The picture below shows someone being "grabbed" by a sticky hand.

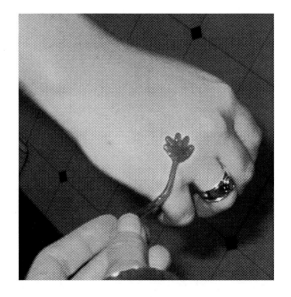

126

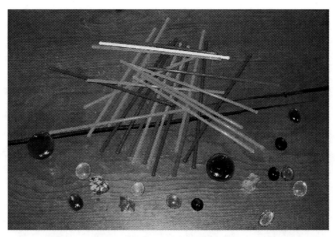

Pick Up Sticks With Attitude

Treatment Modality: Individual/Group/Family
Population: Ages 5 to adult
Treatment Phase: Working

Treatment Goals:
1. To implement soothing self-talk statements
2. To decrease client's self-report of frustration
3. To decrease frequency and intensity of anger outbursts
4. To extend client's frustration tolerance

Props:
Pick-up Sticks™
treasure chest with tokens

Procedure:
This technique has been used most frequently in the group setting. It has been very effective in helping clients learn to control their frustration and stay in the game while at the same time implementing positive self-talk strategies that help them remain calm. Begin by bringing out the game of Pick-Up Sticks™ and explaining the rules. Role play taking a turn. Be sure that a stick moves. In the game, if a stick moves during a

player's attempt to pick up another stick, the player loses his turn. He has made a mistake. Make a mistake with the sticks and pretend to get angry. Ask the clients to guess what the therapist's response will be. The clients will usually say that the therapist is going to "Go off mad," or "Quit the game." Explain how we often stop having fun when we're not winning and how this can spoil the game and our friendships. Talk about the automatic thoughts the client has when he misses a turn. The messages may include "I'm no good." "I can't do anything right." and "I'm always messing up." Explain that in this game, the goal is to stay in the game, even if you make a mistake. Sticks are won when a play is completed without making any of the other sticks move. However, tokens are won, If the player can generate a positive self-talk statement out loud that helps him keep playing. Help the clients generate some of those statements, including, "Oh well, I'll try again next time," and "I'm still learning." "You win some, you lose some," is another example. At the end of the game, tokens and Pick-Up sticks™ count equally towards a prize.

Processing Questions:

What was your first thought when you made a mistake?
How did you feel after you made a mistake?
Is their any connection between what you thought and how you felt?
What were some of the replacement thoughts that helped you keep playing?
How did you feel after you said one of these?
How can you use this new skill in other areas of your life?

Homework Assignment:

The next time that a task frustrates you....like a homework assignment, a game or a chore, use one of the statements that you used in the game to hang in there until the task is completed.

Special Considerations:

Clients who have severe anger outbursts and manifest extreme impulsivity may only be able to do this activity in an individual session with the therapist. In psychiatric hospital settings, where physical safety concerns may be an issue, pick-up stick that have balls on the ends (instead of points) may be substituted.

Applications and Modifications:

One modification to this technique focuses on increasing self-esteem. The name of the game is "Pick Me Up" and every time a participant picks up a stick, she has to say something nice about herself. Both versions of the game can be played in a group setting. In the original version, clients would generate a list together of phrases that they can say to themselves that will help them stay in the game even when they make mistakes and get mad at themselves. In the modified version, clients are instructed to say something that they like about another group member whenever they pick up a stick. They should be encouraged to make eye contact with their peers. The peer being complimented should say thank you and the first person should say you're welcome. This helps clients to work on being good senders and receivers of communication.

Cool As A Cucumber

Treatment Modality: Individual/Group/Family
Population: Ages 3 to adult
Treatment Phase: Working

Treatment Goals:

1. To reduce the frequency and duration of stress reactions
2. To implement relaxation exercises to decrease fear and anger
3. To nurture the client through taking care of her physical body
4. To give the client a concrete image of "calm"

Props:

a refrigerated cucumber, cut into slices and/or prepackaged "cucumber eye pads"
cucumber scented lotion

Procedure:

Although some male clients may be willing to participate in this activity, the female children will love it! Begin by introducing the phrase "Cool as a Cucumber" to the client. Some clients will have already heard of this and will be able to tell you that it means staying unruffled in the midst of upsetting events. Teach this concept and then have the client draw a picture of someone staying as "Cool as a Cucumber" while chaos or fighting or high emotions are happening around them. Explain that the cucumber has a thick skin that protects it's cool middle. Allow the client to sample cucumber slices. Then explain that you are going to "pamper" the client with "cucumber treatments" like they use in the real beauty salon. In order for the cucumber eye pads to be applied the client must close her eyes. Since her eyes will be closed this is the perfect opportunity to have the client practice deep breathing and progressive muscle relaxation. Ask the client if she would like the special cucumber lotion treatment...it makes her skin smell good and feel soft while secretly it is "thickening it" so that other people's angry words can't get through as easily. (The client may request this lotion treatment for several sessions after it is introduced.) Be sure that you ask the child where they would like the lotion applied. It is best to have the parent or caregiver present for this activity because it does involve touch. In lieu of this, consider videotaping the activity in order to show it to the parent later. After the treatments are complete, role play some of the scenarios in which chaos is going on around the child but the child needs to stay calm.. One example of this would be a domestic violence situation.

Processing Questions:

What does it mean to be "cool as a cucumber"?
What relaxation strategies did you use while you had the eye pads on?
How did it feel to have someone apply lotion to you?
When are some times in your own life when it would be helpful to act as "cool as a cucumber"?

Homework Assignment:

Before you go to sleep at night, imagine that you are back in the playroom, wearing your cucumber eye pads. Tense and relax your muscles by taking deep breaths. If parents are supportive co-therapists, have them go through the ritual of applying the cucumber lotion to the child each day, sending the message in metaphor that angry words won't be able to penetrate as deeply anymore.

Special Considerations:

Talk with the client's caregivers regarding any possible allergies the client might have to cucumbers or special lotions. Clients who are survivors of abuse may feel too insecure to close their eyes with the therapist...or may not want their bodies touched due to previous violations. Honor the child's boundaries. These concerns can often be handled by having a supportive caregiver in the room during the whole activity. Also, the child can decide to keep her eyes open and apply the lotion herself.

Applications and Modifications:

Although the above section speaks to the difficulties that survivors of abuse may have with this technique, it is my strong opinion that these children need positive nurturing touch more than any other children. The pampering, nurturing quality of this activity combined with the relaxation training that is given make it a perfect technique for use with survivors of abuse. This technique can also be used in family sessions. One family member applies lotion to another, until everyone in the family has had this experience. The phrase "cool as a cucumber" can become part of the family's repertoire of verbal prompts that remind family members to relax and counter escalation in stressful situations.

The Bubble Fall

Treatment Modality: Individual/Group/Family
Population: Ages 3 to adults
Treatment Phase: Working

Treatment Goals:
1. To decrease the intensity and duration of stress reactions
2. To give the client a focal point to help in relaxation training
3. To practice deep breathing
4. To practice progressive muscle tensing/relaxing

Props:
bubbles
soft music

Procedure:
This technique is very simple, yet soothing. After the initial phase of therapy is successfully navigated and the client has established trust with the therapist, the therapist can begin to introduce specific relaxation exercises. In my experience, young children have some difficulty with free flowing relaxation techniques. Some children are able to use their imaginations well, others are traumatized by nightmare images that invade their daytime imaginings. Moreover, some children, due to an abusive home life, don't feel safe enough to close their eyes at all. It was with these factors in mind that I began using bubbles in relaxation work.

Begin the activity by asking the child to get comfortable (lean back in her chair, lay down on the floor, etc). Turn on some soft music and ask the client to focus on this. Before blowing the bubbles, warn the client that bubbles are going to begin to fall around her. The clients job is simply to choose one bubble at a time and watch it fall. The technique is particularly effective if the client is willing to lie down on the floor, because then she can track the bubbles all the way from the height at which they were blown to the point at which they burst (which is often when they come to rest gently on the child). Children who have trouble concentrating and who wriggle around during other relaxation exercises are able to remain very still during the Bubble Fall, because they have a visual stimulus attached to the relaxation process. The therapist can also take the client through a full body muscle tension and relaxation exercise as the bubbles are falling. If this technique is practiced often enough, the client begins to associate the visual stimulus "bubbles" with the kinesthetic act of relaxing.

Processing Questions:
Were you able to track the bubbles until they popped?
How did it feel to watch the bubbles fall?
Were you able to think of other things as you watched the bubbles? Why or why not?
What are some situations in which it would help you to pretend the bubbles are falling?

Homework Assignment:
When you get into bed each night for the next week, spend one minute imagining the bubbles falling while trying to relax. (If there are supportive caregivers in the home, the assignment could be for the parents to blow bubbles over the child for one to three minutes before bedtime, as a relaxation routine.)

Special Considerations:
Children who have experienced abuse of any kind may have difficulty relaxing at all. It may feel like a loosening of the defenses when they have previously had to be on guard for their psychological survival. The technique may need to be introduced later in the therapy process for these clients.

Applications and Modifications:

This technique can *be used* over and over again. It can *become* part of the child's arsenal in fighting fear, anger outbursts, worry, *bedtime*, etc. It can *be* integrated into every session, as a closing activity (particularly when trauma work has *been* done) to help clients prepare for their return to the "real world". The Bubble Fall is particularly helpful when the therapist is practicing in a school *based* setting, where children are often faced with situations in which they could potentially escalate several times a day. The therapist and the client can come up with a "code word" that will help the client quickly visualize the *bubbles*. Due to the physiological relaxation response that has *been* kinesthetically paired with the Bubble Fall over and over again in the playroom, the word trigger can help the client de-escalate quickly and avoid an altercation. Of course, it is helpful to role play the integration of the Bubble Fall into everyday life through *use* of puppets, etc. in the playroom. When the client "graduates" from therapy, you can give her a container of *bubbles* by which to remember the relaxation work (and practice at home).

Soothing Bottles

Treatment Modality: Group/Family

Population: Ages 2 to 7

Treatment Phase: Working

Treatment Goals:

1. To implement relaxation training
2. To provide a cognitive and visual distraction during de-escalation
3. To decrease the frequency, intensity and duration of tantrums
4. To provide client with a security object

Props:

plastic water or coke bottles
water
food coloring
glitter
special stones (like those used in flower vases)
cooking oil
other objects as needed bauble or special symbol that has meaning for

Procedure:

Begin by talking about different ways that we get upset.
Explain that we also have different ways of calming back down.

Sometimes people take deep breaths, sometimes they count to ten, and other times they find something to stare at, to distract them, until the "upset feeling" goes away. Introduce all the materials to the client and say "We're going to make a cool bottle for you to hold on to, look at and play with when you need to "chill out" or calm down. (Bottles are very soothing and almost all children associate bottles with nurture and sustenance and safety.) It works best to use water bottles that hold sixteen ounces or less, so that tiny hands can hold onto them. The client begins by putting some water in the bottle (but leave a lot of room for any objects she may want to add. Show the client the food color containers and help her add the desired amount until her liquid is the color that is most soothing for her. This may vary from bright pink to light blue. Just make sure that she will still be able to see the objects through the water. The client is then encouraged to add stones, sequins, glitter, etc. to the bottle. There may be a symbol or a metaphor that you and the client have already used extensively...like a sun, or a rainbow. A tiny waterproof version of the object available can be made available for the client to add to her bottle. Oil can also be added. Since it separates from water, it will provide more visual stimulation for the child as the child turns it upside down and right side up again. The bottle can be described as the client's very own "snow globe" to help them "chill out". Several versions of real snow globes can be brought as models for the client. Be sure that the client practices focusing on the bottle when she gets upset.

Processing Questions:

What did you choose to put in your bottle and why?
Tell me a story about what happens in the world inside your bottle?
When are some times that you might use your bottle?

Homework Assignment:

Spend time each day just looking at your bottle and taking deep breaths. If you like, you can make up new adventures about what goes on inside the world you've created in the bottle. One time this week, when you feel yourself getting angry with a friend, go get your bottle and use it to calm down.

Special Considerations:

Be very careful to seal the top of the bottle in some way. (You can actually melt the plastic lid to the top of the bottle.) Avoid creating a choking hazards. If the bottle gets damaged in some way, it should be thrown away immediately. The therapist and child can then make a new one.

Applications and Modifications:

Although the bottles are designed primarily as a concrete tool to help clients calm down when they begin to get angry or upset, they can also function as transitional objects for when the client cannot be with the therapist. They can function like security blankets. Many preschool age children will ask to take them to their cots for naptime. I always encourage this, because the child is more likely to fall asleep if they have a security object with them. They are more likely to rest quietly if they have a constantly changing visual image to look at. The therapist can even encourage the client to make up a story about what happens in the world inside the bottle...try to steer these stories to safe, happy endings.

This technique can also be done in group settings, with all participants making their bottles at the same time. This is also an excellent technique to use in family work with clients who suffer from separation anxiety. Help the client and parent to create a bottle together. The parent might add a piece of old jewelry to the bottle, so that the child has something of mommy's or daddy's inside the bottle. Then the family can make up a story about the bottle that highlights the connection between parent and child even when the parent is away. The story should also send a clear message that the parent will always come back.

Self-Control Strategies

140

The Awkward Octopus

Treatment Modality: Individual/Group

Population: Ages 3 to adults

Treatment Phase: Working/Termination

Treatment Goals:

1. To highlight the consequences of impulsive behavior
2. To generate alternative strategies to impulsive touching
3. To practice through role play new impulse control skills
4. To increase social skills

Props:

several octopus puppets
index cards
safety pins
markers

Procedure:

Using an octopus puppet, begins by telling a story about an octopus who was always getting into trouble because he was always touching things and people that he shouldn't. It was just so difficult for him, because he had eight arms. That's a lot more to keep up with than most of his friends, who were fish and didn't have any arms at all, just fins. He would *see* a shiny orange fish and one of his eight arms would reach out and touch it *before* he remembered that he is supposed to ask first. This kind of thing was always happening." Ask the client if this kind of thing ever happens to him. Help the client to generate scenarios in which his own impulsivity gets him into trouble. In the story, the octopus thinks of a good idea. He thinks, I will write reminders on each of my arms. I'm *bound* to see it the reminder as I'm reaching out to touch things. Then I'll avoid getting into trouble. The reminder will also list a helpful way to keep my hands to myself." Tell the client that the octopus needs help brainstorming coping strategies for helping the octopus keep his hands to himself. Each time a useful idea is generated, the client writes it down on an index card (or draws a picture of it) and the therapist pins it to one arm (leg?)of the puppet. After each new technique is pinned to the octopus, the client gets to "be" the octopus puppet and practice the new skill.

Processing Questions:
What was the octopus' problem?
How did this problem make the octopus feel?
What did he do to help himself?
Describe some of the coping strategies the octopus learned to keep his hands to himself.
What are some situations in your own life where you could use these same strategies?

Homework Assignment:
Practice self-control one time per day using one of the strategies that we taught to the octopus. Be sure to use several different strategies over the course of a week. Be prepared to talk about which ones worked best.

Special Considerations:

For children who are diagnosed ADD, the completion and practice of this technique may not be possible until a medication trial is underway due to the level of concentration that is required to complete the activity. Therefore, I would suggest the use of this technique in conjunction with medication management.

Applications and Modifications:

This is a great technique for skill-building related to self-control. Clients love the universalization that occurs as they listen to the story about the octopus who can't control himself. Moreover, clients feel like the octopus must be in worse shape than they are, because although the clients have trouble controlling their two arms and two legs...the octopus has twice this many. This comparison places the client naturally in the role of the helper (kids love this). It may seem like overkill to generate eight coping strategies (these can also include simple "Stop and Think" statements that the octopus would say to himself), but children will complete the activity, because they are motivated by getting to use the puppet, the sense of altruism that comes from helping the octopus and the sense of mastery that they begin to feel as they practice the new skills (in the guise of the octopus).

The group setting lends itself well to the use of this technique. The clients all listen together to the story and then take turns generating coping strategies and getting to practice as the octopus. The octopus (with all the coping strategies attached) can remain a visual figure in the room. It can be referred to as impulse control problems arise.

The Awkward Octopus
(an example)

The above picture shows several different octopus puppets that can be used for this activity. In the picture, "The Awkward Octopus" has had two strategies for keeping his hands and feet to himself pinned to him already. The clients take turns using the octopus puppet and practicing, through role play, the application of these coping strategies.

Freeze Bowl

Treatment Modality: Group/Family
Population: Ages 3 to adult
Treatment Phase: Working

Treatment Goals:

1. To increase attention span
2. To increase self-control
3. To decrease impulsivity

Props:

miniature set of bowling pins
miniature bowling ball
digital timers
tokens

Procedure:

Begin by issuing a challenge to the clients...How long can they freeze? Explain that freezing means being completely still. Tell the clients that you are going to play a game which will require freezing. Set up the bowling pins on a low table, or in the middle of the floor. You and the children will need to come up with a ratio of "freeze time" per pin knocked over. This ratio can vary greatly depending on the age and clinical issues faced by your clients. For example, two seconds per pin might be the ratio for a four year old. If a child knocks down three pins on her turn, she would have to freeze for six seconds (two seconds times three). Six seconds is a long time for some four year olds. With the mini bowling ball sets and the short distance between the child and the pins, the child is likely to knock over five or six (which would equal ten or twelve seconds). The number of seconds of freeze time represented by each pin will be higher for older children. For example, the ratio might be five seconds per pin for a group of ten year olds. However, if the ten year olds in question have all been diagnosed with severe Attention Deficit Disorder, they may need to be assigned the same time frame that is used for four year old clients, to account for the inattention and impulsivity. Once a time frame has been decided upon, each participant gets a practice round, during which all the other group members must watch carefully to see if the bowler moves at all. An easy way to keep track of the time is to use digital timers or stopwatches. Once a group member has bowled and knocked down her pins, set the timer. The group member may move when her timer reaches zero. (This also encourages self-monitoring.) The therapist may need several digital timers if players are taking turns rapidly. An alternative strategy would be to pair two group members together. This is a great strategy for Oppositional Defiant Disordered children because the better they work together and the more they encourage each other, the more points they can earn. In this scenario, one partner has the timer while the other one is freezing and then they switch. Each time that the child is able to freeze for the amount of time calculated based on how many pins were knocked down, she gets a token. At the end of the game, each child who has earned a certain number of tokens gets a prize (make sure that the number needed to win a prize is reachable by everyone). This game can create a lot of excitement and it is fast paced, but that is part of why it is such a powerful training tool for children with self-control issues. Every time they are able to freeze for the required length of time to earn a token, their self-esteem and their sense of their own competency goes up.

146

Processing Questions:

Were you able to hold the freeze for the required length of time?

How did it feel when you were able to do it?

What skills did you have to use to hold the freeze?

What happened on the turns where you were not able to hold the freeze? What got in your way?

Are there any situations in your life, where freezing (remaining still for a length of time) might be helpful?

Homework Assignment:

Look at the clock in your classroom and "hold a freeze" in your seat for five seconds. Try to remain so still that no one even notices you're there. (Coach the child on how to decide which part of the class day would be a good time to try this.) Be prepared to talk about the experience.

Special Considerations:

Clients who are easily distracted may have a hard time completing a freeze simply because they begin watching the next player and get swept up in the excitement. It may be necessary to stop and process after the first round. Help these clients develop strategies (like closing their eyes or repeating the word "freeze" inside their heads over and over again) for remaining still despite the distractions. (This technique can be used in conjunction with "Count the Cost", another technique designed to help clients focus and tune out outside stimuli.)

Applications and Modifications:

This technique works best in a group setting, because the competition motivates clients to work harder at controlling themselves. Families could also benefit from this technique. All family members play the game and then the metaphor of freezing, once practiced, can be used as a fun way to prompt children to pay attention and use self-control at home. A token economy system can be worked out for the home that involves tokens in exchange for "freezing" when directed.

The metaphor can be internalized and clients can practice "freezing" internally before engaging in impulsive actions. Examples of this can be generated and role played with puppets.

Pictured above is an inexpensive, miniature plastic bowling set. Hanging behind the bowling set is a stopwatch which can be used to time the clients' freeze poses.

148

Conducting Chaos

Treatment Modality: Group

Population: Ages 4 to adult

Treatment Phase: Beginning/Working

Treatment Goals:

1. To increase concentration
2. To lengthen attention span
3. To increase impulse control

Props:

2 pieces of felt or construction paper (a different color for each participant)
musical instruments

Procedure:

One group member is chosen to be the "conductor". The rest of the group members are part of the orchestra. Each orchestra member gets a piece of colored paper or felt and a musical instrument. One might have a piece of blue felt and maracas. The conductor gets the second piece of paper or felt in every color represented in the orchestra. The conductor holds up various colors and the orchestra members must begin to play their instruments when their color is held up and stop playing immediately (this is usually the challenging part for clients) when their color is put back down. To play the game well, participants must follow non-verbal directions, pay close attention, tune out other stimuli and control their impulses. Each member of the group should get a turn to be the conductor.

Processing Questions:

What did you like about being the conductor (being in charge)?
What was hard or frustrating about being the conductor?
What did you like about being in the orchestra (taking direction, working as a team)?
What was hard for you about being in the orchestra?
Which role did you like better and why?
What skills did orchestra members need to make music.

Homework Assignment:

After processing how group members took non-verbal directions, have them keep a log of non-verbal directions that they are given by teachers, parents and even peers. For example, a peer who is tired of listening to you may turn his gaze elsewhere. This may be a non-verbal direction (clue) for you to change the subject.

Special Considerations:

If you have one child in the group who cannot control his impulses and always plays out of turn, consequences should be provided. However, the peer feedback that he will receive from his frustrated conductor and fellow group members will also help to create therapeutic change in this pattern.

150

Applications and Modifications:

This technique is great for use in groups that include children diagnosed with ADD, ODD and other impulse control disorders. It is especially useful as an introduction to the concept of non-verbal cues and directions. If felt or colored paper is not available another material can be used, as long as two objects of the same color are available to every participant (two Lego's, two crayons, etc.) If musical instruments are hard to come by, group members can simply create a unique sound and rhythm and produce them when their colors are raised.

Count The Cost

Treatment Modality: Group
Population: Ages 6 to adult
Treatment Phase: Working

Treatment Goals:
1. To increase attention span
2. To increase the client's ability to focus
3. To practice blocking out non-essential stimuli

Props:
a miniature deck of cards

Procedure:
Begin by asking the group members if they ever get distracted...especially when they're supposed to be focusing. Have the clients generate a list of what kinds of behaviors or situations call for intense focus (examples include taking a test, trying to win a video game, cutting up food, using scissors, etc.). Have the clients generate another list of the kinds of behaviors or situations that tend to distract them from their tasks (examples include someone making a loud noise, someone insulting them, people playing when they are working, etc.). Introduce the concept of cost. It costs something to maintain your focus...it's expensive, it requires expending energy and it doesn't always come easily. In this game, each client gets a

turn to be the one "who counts the cost". Take the miniature deck of cards and count them once. Then ask the group, "Not too hard, right? Well, what if everybody else is trying to distract me...throw me off?. I have to work extra hard to focus and it costs a lot more energy than just counting the cards in quiet costs."

To win a round, the client with the cards must count them out loud continuously while keeping her eyes on the cards. The client cannot stop counting or look up from the cards. When the client gets to 52, she wins. (You can modify the number of cards that have to be counted depending on the age and capabilities of your particular group.) The rest of the group is supposed to try to distract the card counter and make that person interrupt himself. However, rules *must* be decided upon regarding what the" peanut gallery" can do to distract the card counter. In most situations, they should not be allowed to touch the card counter in any way, or use any curse words of any kind. You may add whatever additional limits seem appropriate for your population. Many children do not succeed at this the first time. After everyone has had a turn, process the experience, highlighting strategies that worked for retaining focus and offering new strategies. The game should be played until everyone has had an experience of success. Another aspect of the game is that the card counter may become very frustrated with herself or angry with her peers for the ways in which they try to distract her. It is important that these feelings be processed and that clients practice channeling these feelings into aggressive concentration.

Processing Questions:

How did it feel to try to count while others were distracting you?

What strategies did you have to use to stay focused?

How did it feel to accomplish the task?

How did it feel to be one of the people trying to distract the card counter?

What are some times and places in your life where this level of concentration would be helpful?

Homework Assignment:

Find some other people to practice this game with, either family or friends, before you come for your next session. Be prepared to discuss how it went.

Special Considerations:

Clients with Attention Deficit Disorder, Impulse Control Disorder, Oppositional Defiant Disorder and Conduct Disorder may have a particularly hard time with this game...either because of the attentional skills required, or because of the frustration and anger that can be generated. The therapist will need to be extra supportive with some of these children...even to the point of standing in the middle with them and counting out loud with them. Another possibility is to pair a child who has attentional difficulties with one who is high functioning in this area.

Applications and Modifications:

This technique requires many distracters, and therefore lends itself to the group setting. Although I have the focusing participant count cards, you can substitute lots of other activities...as long as the client has to repeat a behavior continually while keeping his head down.

This technique can also be modified to address study habits with individual clients. The therapist can give the client a task and then blast a television set or radio, rustle candy wrappers or crunch potato chips. Afterwards, the therapist can help the child design a "study environment" and a schedule, with snack times and breaks planned away from the study area. In order to succeed at the game, the client has to repeatedly ignore others' attempts to distract her. Ignoring, a skill that can be very hard for children when they are being teased, can be painted as a powerful tool through this activity.

154

Lock Your Lips

Treatment Modality: Individual/Group/Family
Population: Ages 5 to adult
Treatment Phase: Working

Treatment Goals:
1. To develop self-control
2. To decrease impulsivity
3. To increase the client's ability to listen to directions and complete tasks

Props:
lip gloss
chapstick
paper
markers/crayons
magic wand
magician's hat or puppet

Procedure:
Many of the clients that we see have impulse control problems. These clients are likely to shout out in class, talk to peers when they should be working, and respond to insults from peers with

insults of their own *before* they stop and think. This technique is designed to address these issues. Begin by talking about ways that our mouths can get us into trouble. Pose the question, "Wouldn't it *be* nice if there was a magic potion that could seal our lips when we're not supposed to *be* using them?" Explain that the client is going to create his own magic lip wand. The client is presented with a lip gloss of her very own, this technique will work with male clients too, as long as a transparent chapstick is used. Many of the male clients I *see* view it as a privilege to have their "very own chapstick" to take care of their lips (particularly during the winter months). The therapist gives the client a very small piece of paper (just *big* enough to wrap around the chapstick and invites her to name her magic lip wand. The name is written on the paper and taped around the chapstick. The client is then encouraged to don the magician's cap, take the magic wand and cast a spell over the chapstick or lip gloss, so that it has magical powers to lock her lips. Help the client come up with real life scenarios in which staying quiet would *be* helpful. The therapist tries everything she can think of to get the client to talk, but (after the client applies the chapstick) the client will not *be* moved. If the client begins to feel like she might talk, she should apply another coating of the magic chapstick.

Processing Questions:

What are some ways in which your lips can get you into trouble?
What is one way to take control over your lips?
How do you decide when your lips should *be* locked?
In what situations could it *be* helpful to have your lips locked?

Homework Assignment:

Use your magic lip wand one time in class and one time at home each day when you feel like talking and you're not supposed to. Try using it to keep from responding to a peer who is teasing you.

Special Considerations:

The therapist must be careful to explain this technique and the rationale for using it with this client to teachers and parents alike. Any use of the chapstick as a reminder for the client not to talk in the classroom must first be cleared with the teacher. Many teachers are understanding about these kinds of props. However, if the child is not allowed to take the chapstick into the classroom, the therapist will have to help the client internalize the metaphor through more guided imagery and visualization work.

Applications and Modifications:

This technique can be used with children who may need to disclose ongoing abuse of some kind. In this case, the magician puppet would cast an evil spell on the magic lip wand, come into the child's room when she is sleeping and apply it to her lips. In the morning, the child would want to tell things that have happened but her lips are locked. The therapist and client would then come up with ways to break the evil wizard's spell and unlock the child's lips. This technique can be done in a group format and also with families. In fact, in the family system, the chapstick could end up being used as a non-verbal cue to the child regarding appropriate times to stop talking.

Techniques for Working with Survivors of Abuse

158

The Landing Tray

Treatment Modality: Individual/Group/Family

Population: Ages 3 to adults

Treatment Phase: Beginning/Working/Termination

Treatment Goals:

1. To learn a relaxation exercise
2. To be able to generate guided imagery when needed
3. To decrease client's perception of stress and/or anger
4. To give the therapist projective information re: client's psyche

Props:

Where Do Balloons Go? by Jamie Lee Curtis
one balloon per participant
sandtray
miniatures
clay (to make any additional symbols that aren't in your collection of miniatures)

Procedure:

Begin by reading the book Where Do Balloons Go? aloud. Ask the clients to close their eyes and imagine being the balloons in the book. Instruct the clients to pretend to go where the balloons go in the story. After the book has been read, Ask each client to pick out a balloon to represent himself. It is important to have a wide variety of balloons in many different shapes, colors and sizes. Then ask each child to imagine where they would land if they were a balloon. Present a whole guided imagery exercise, in which the client is lifted away from the playground by a strong wind. Help the client experience floating through the air, way above everything and everyone. Storms come and toss the balloon around. Finally, instruct the client to visualize landing in a safe place. The child is given a sandtray and access to the miniatures. The client is then asked to create the "world" in which his balloon landed in the sandtray. Process the tray. After the tray has been processed, instruct the client to create a story about the balloon and the other objects in the sandtray world. If the exercise is used in a group setting, all other members listen and are encouraged to ask questions about the world. It is possible to glean much projective information from this technique.

Processing Questions:
How did it feel to be a balloon floating through the air?
How did it feel to land?
Tell me about this place.
How does the balloon feel in this place?
What will happen to the balloon in this place?
Is there any other place that the balloon would like to be?
Where? Why?

Homework Assignment:
One time this week, when you start to feel yourself getting angry or stressed out (like before a test or when someone says something ugly to you), bring back the picture in your mind of being a balloon floating through the air. Pretend that you are far away. Be prepared to report on how the picture in your head helped you handle the situation.

Special Considerations:

Older children might find the book "childish", so just be sure you know your population before you use this technique. Because of the uses of guided imagery to induce relaxation, this technique might not be the best fit for children suffering from any form of psychosis. Children who have suffered from abuse may not be able to land their balloons in a safe place.

Applications and Modifications:

This technique can be used in individual sessions or in a group setting. In my experience, the child often reports feeling safe and light floating through the air, but often lands in a war zone and feels trapped or bound for destruction. This is a reflection of the level of danger and helplessness she senses in her current environment. If this happens with your clients, you should validate their feelings, process the tray and then ask the last processing question: "Is there any other place that the balloon would like to be?" Allow them to create another sandtray...you can even become fairly directive and say..."This doesn't seem like a safe place for this balloon to stay...so let's pretend that a great big powerful wind comes along and picks up the balloon and drops it back down into a much safer place. Take some time to show me, in a new sandtray, what the much safer place looks like.

This technique can be adapted for a termination activity, by having the client imagine and then create a sandtray depicting where he wants to "end up" or "land" in life. This can be used to begin a conversation about long-term goals and how to reach them.

The Landing Tray
(an example)

In this tray the balloon lands in a place that has a dangerous beast. However, many protective characters are placed around the beast and serve as a shield between the beast and the balloon. The powerful Hercules stands guard in front of the balloon and a nurturing mother with baby stands beside the balloon. The ground surrounding the balloon is covered in treasures. The tray ultimately reflects a person who sees the dangers around him, but has protective buffers from those dangers. If the balloon had landed in a place where the beast was creating destruction, the tray would be thoroughly explored and then the client would be encouraged to change the tray in some way that gives the balloon more protection.

162

"Zip It"

Treatment Modality: Individual/Group
Population: Ages 4 to adult
Treatment Phase: Working

Treatment Goals:

1. To create safety for the client
2. To relieve pressure to talk about the abuse immediately
3. To begin to desensitize clients to "the secret"
4. To honor the client's silence

Props:

animal puppets whose mouths are made of zippers (or)
animal change purses with zippers

Procedure:

Many children come to treatment with secrets to tell. We, as therapists must earn the right to hear those secrets. Therapy should create a holding environment for a child, and part of that holding may include very literally holding secrets for them. I recently acquired an alligator puppet whose teeth are the two threads of a zipper. Many times, children's mouths are sealed. Sometimes, a perpetrator has threatened to hurt the child or someone the child cares about if she tells. Sometimes the client feels incredible shame and believes she must be bad for this to be happening to her. Therefore, she must tell no one. It is important that we honor the child's silence at the same time that we recognize that one of the ultimate goals is full disclosure.

Begin by telling the client that everyone has secrets. Some secrets are things that children don't want anyone else to know (like they have candy hidden under their beds). Other secrets are things that children really want helpful adults to know, but they are afraid to tell. Whatever the reason, the secrets stay inside. If the painful secrets stay inside, they start to feel bigger and bigger and worse and worse. Ask the client to think of one of their painful secrets and write it down. you're going to feed it to one of these animals." After the child has written it down, explain to him that he is going to feed it to an animal. Inform the client that these animals are special because their mouths zip shut. These animals are very good at keeping secrets. Ask the client which animal looks to him like it's the best at keeping a secret. Have him put his secret in that animal's mouth and zip it up tight. Tell the client, "Your secret will stay there until you are ready to show it to me." In this way, the burden of the secret can be psychologically placed on the animal (at least in part). (If you have several of the zip able animal change purses, you can assign this one to this client for as long as it takes for her to share the secret with you.) Here's where it gets tricky. If the child has written on her secret, "My daddy comes in my room every night and rapes me." the therapist needs to act on this information as soon as possible. However, the secret might be about something that is shameful to the child but not particularly harmful, in an immediate sense, or perhaps the secret does describe abuse, but it is abuse that has already been documented and the child is now in a safe place. What I would do "just in case" is explain to the child after she has zipped her secret into the animal, that these animals have known and loved lots of children. These animals believe that it is their first job to protect children and their second job to keep secrets. So if the animal decides that the secret is something that is putting the client in immediate danger, the animal will show the secret to the therapist...but the animal will guard all other secrets with its life.

Processing Questions:

List all the different kinds of secrets that people can have.
What kind of secret is yours?
How has it felt to carry around the secret inside?
How does it feel to give the secret to the animal?
Imagine what it would be like to tell the secret that you placed inside the animal...what does it feel like to think about doing that?

Homework Assignment:

When you start to feel the weight of your secret, remember that you have already "told" once by feeding it to the animal and nothing bad happened. Know that the secret is ready whenever you want to unzip the animal's mouth and share it with me.

Special Considerations:

Children with writing deficits or children who are too young to write might be frustrated by this exercise. They might feel put in a bind because they can't write it down without help...which would mean sharing their secret verbally with the therapist, which they are not ready to do. The alternative for these children is to simply have them whisper the secret to the animal. Because animals can't talk and even if they could these animals' lips are zipped, the animal won't repeat the client's secret. This can be used as practice and desensitization to eventually telling the therapist the secret.

Applications and Modifications:

This technique was originally designed for use with survivors of sexual abuse...and for use with children who might have been abused. but have not made a disclosure yet. However, an alternate use of this technique can be made with children who have impulse control problems and with clients who get in trouble for talking too much or talking out of turn. The zip able puppets can be used in this context to practice "zipping your lips" in appropriate circumstances.

Another application of this technique would be to teach children who "shut down" when they've done something wrong that it's better in the long run to go ahead and "unzip" or tell the truth now and face the consequence than it is to "zip up" about it and make the caregiver even angrier. These children end up with one consequence for the original misbehavior and another for refusing to speak about it. The zip able puppets can be used to role play both of the above scenarios. The original technique should only be used in individual sessions, but the two modifications can be used in a group or family session.

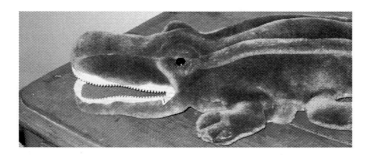

The above picture shows an alligator puppet. It's mouth is made out of a zipper. Here it is open, ready to be filled with secrets. Below is the alligator after a child has zipped her secret in its mouth.

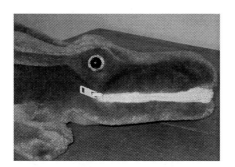

The Creep and The Creepy Crawlies

Treatment Modality: Individual
Population: Ages 3 to adult
Treatment Phase: Working

Treatment Goals:
1. To decrease the client's secrecy surrounding sexual abuse
2. To move the client closer to a verbal description of the abuse
3. To express feelings about the abuse and himself through art
4. To place responsibility for the abuse on the perpetrator

Props:
blank paper
markers/ crayons
spider stickers

Procedure:
Begin this technique by normalizing the experience of uncomfortable feelings related to touch. Explain to the client, "Everybody has ways that they like to be touched and ways that they don't like to be touched. When a child is touched in a way he doesn't like or on a part of her body that he doesn't want touched, we call those creepy crawly touches. Sometimes it is hard to talk about creepy crawly touches...exactly because they feel so creepy. But the real creep is the person who touched

you in a way you didn't like. Have the child draw a self-portrait (this part of the activity alone should give you plenty of information about the client's self-perceptions). Introduce the spider stickers. Spider stickers that have a transparent background and black spiders seem to be the most effective. (When the transparent stickers are applied to the drawn body, they look like real spiders crawling around instead of stickers defined by the outline of their background.) When the client has finished the self-portrait, invite him to apply a spider sticker to any part of his body, in the drawing, that has ever been made to feel creepy crawly. I generated this technique after working with a 10 year old boy with Asperger's-like symptoms who had been sexually abused. He refused to make eye contact with me, much less use his words to verbalize any of the abuse. The perpetrator had confessed and the client's non-offending parent was fully supportive of the child talking, but he refused. He really liked the spider stickers though, and wanted an opportunity to play with them. This motivation was enough for him to complete the activity. However, he folded the paper over and over again, and put it in my lockbox, under many army men, grenades, tanks, etc. I wasn't allowed to look at it for several more sessions. However, the client was taking baby steps towards verbally disclosing the abuse through applying the stickers to his self-portrait.

Processing Questions:

How do you think the person in the picture feels with those spiders crawling on her?
Who let the spiders get on the person?
What does the person in the drawing want to happen?
Is there any way to get the spiders off?

Homework Assignment:

Be aware that the therapist will keep this picture in your special file. Every time you think of the creepy crawlies...say to yourself "He's the creep, not me!"

168

Special Considerations:

Survivors of *sexual abuse* must *be* handled carefully in treatment. If this technique is not used in the right phase of therapy, it could end up retraumatizing the child. Be sure that the client has already *begun* to address issue related to *blame* and *self-worth*. Also *be* sure that the responsibility has already *been* placed with the perpetrator through *several* different play therapy metaphors *before* this technique is introduced.

Applications and Modifications:

After the perpetrator has *been* characterized as the creep who brings the creep crawlies, the phrase "the creep" may *be* used in consequent sessions instead of the perpetrator's name. Sometimes this layer of removal makes it easier for the child to talk about what happened. The technique is intended to *be* part of a progression from showing to telling about the abuse. The client draws the picture and places the spiders. This may *be* his first clear communication that something awful has happened to him. He realizes that he is not punished and the world does not fall apart because he "showed". This increases his motivation to "tell" about the abuse. In cases where the abuse has already *been* documented, the child should get to decide when the non-offending parent or other caregiver gets to see the picture. If this creepy crawly exercise is part of an assessment, then any resultant concerning information should *be* shared with the proper authorities.

An important modification is to give the client the option of creating a story or drawing in which the spiders get removed. Survivors of *sexual abuse* need the empowerment that comes with getting rid of the spiders.

The Creep and The Creepy Crawlies
(an example)

The above picture is an example of a client being able to show the parts of her body on which "creepy crawlies" appeared. Working from this picture, the client was then able to go into detailed verbal debriefing of the traumatic events. This client also added other stickers to represent other feelings.

Finding Your Voice

Treatment Modality: Individual

Population: Ages 3 to 10

Treatment Phase: Working

Treatment Goals:

1. To normalize the experience of being unable to tell about abuse
2. To normalize the experience of being shy or unable to say what you want to say
3. To give clients an opportunity to practice telling the secret
4. To increase social skills

Props:

The Very Quiet Cricket by Eric Carle
cricket toy that chirps
cricket finger puppets

Procedure:

Begin by reading The Very Quiet Cricket. This beautiful book is the story of a baby cricket who keeps meeting new insects. All of the insects talk to him and he tries to respond, but he is unable to find his voice. At the end of every page, Carle writes "But nothing happened. Not a sound." The little cricket wants so badly to speak, but can't get the words out. At the very end of the book, the cricket meets another cricket like himself and is able to make "the most beautiful sound" that the other cricket had ever heard. After reading the story, ask the client, "Can you think of a situation in which you felt like this little cricket?" The therapist may be able to be more directive, if, for example, abuse charges have already been substantiated. In this case, the metaphor becomes about the powerful forces that kept the child from telling. The healing metaphor comes when the cricket is finally able to speak. Have the child write down what she wanted or wants to say to the perpetrator, to other caregivers. etc. If there is any possibility of ongoing abuse, this intervention may encourage the child to tell. Ask the child to write down any thing that she would like to say but can't (like the cricket). Read the story again, but this time give the client the stuffed cricket with the voice box inside. When the final page is reached, the client can act out the cricket finally making a sound by pressing on the voice box within the stuffed cricket. If the client is comfortable with all of this, then she can invited to take the intervention to the next level, which is practicing (with the cricket finger puppet) the statement(s) she would really like to make if she could talk to the perpetrator, the non-protecting parent, another victim, etc. Eventually the client may feel empowered enough to write a letter to the perpetrator or verbally confront a non-protecting parent with the therapist present. Each progressive acting out of the cricket chirping encourages the client that it will become possible for her to speak as well.

Processing Questions:

How do you think the cricket felt when he couldn't make a sound?

What had to happen for him to finally learn how to talk?

How do you think the cricket felt after he made "the most beautiful sound"?

What factors keep you from talking when you want to?

What's one thing that you really want to tell someone, but you can't?

Homework Assignment:

If the technique is being used with a survivor of abuse, instruct the client to do the following: Write down one thing you would like to say to the person who hurt you and let the therapist keep it in a special place for you. If the technique is being used with clients who suffer from shyness instruct the client to do the following: Say hello to one person that you usually don't greet. An alternate assignment is: Ask one person to play a game with you this week.

Special Considerations:

Older children might find the book "childish", so just be sure you know your population before you use this technique. This technique can work well for survivors of abuse, but be careful not to push these children too hard. Be careful not to set a child up for failure. For example, having a child tell his teacher, "I feel like you ignore me." if the teacher is going to laugh at her will defeat the point of practicing the use of her voice.

Applications and Modifications:

There are as many applications of this technique as there are children to treat. Every child (and adult for that matter) is in the process of discovering his/her voice. This technique can be used to equip a child to say something important, to diffuse anger, to make a fear manageable, etc. The metaphor of breaking the silence is particularly powerful in the treatment of children with Selective Mutism.

The second processing question is "What had to happen for the cricket to finally learn how to talk?" It took another cricket (a female cricket)...one of its own kind. The metaphor can be made to reflect the fact that a child client needs to know that there are other people like her. She must feel a commonality of some sort in order to be able to open up. This technique is particularly powerful with children who suffer from extreme shyness. The cricket finger puppet can be used to practice statements for joining a group, saying hello, asking someone to play with her, etc. Another client might have anger issues. This technique can be used to help the child practice using her words to talk about her anger.

The above picture shows one example of a cricket with a voice box inside.

Change the Channel

Treatment Modality: Individual/Family
Population: Ages 3 to adult
Treatment Phase: Working

Treatment Goals:
1. To explore or process scary images
2. To help clients experience some level of control over frightening images
3. To decrease nightmares or waking flashbacks

Props:
cardboard box
tinfoil
paper
markers
remote control

Procedure:
This is a wonderful activity for children because it ties images from nightmares and flashbacks, that can be very hard for children to process verbally, to concrete objects with which they come into contact daily. Almost every child has contact with television sets and remote controls from a very early age. Toddlers enjoy playing with the remote control because the grown ups are always doing it (and it has all those cool

buttons).   Once the toddler figures out that pressing a button makes an immediate change in the picture or sound of the T.V., they will do it over and over again.   Why?   It is an immediate cause and effect scenario.   They are having an impact on their environment and experiencing self-efficacy.

The child who is suffering from nightmares or waking flashbacks often feels helpless to do anything about them. They describe themselves as being at the "whim" of the dreams.   This technique is meant to empower these clients.

Begin by having the client draw a picture of a nightmare that he often experiences.   After this picture is processed, the therapist encourages the client to change the nightmare in a way that "takes the power out of it" or makes it "not so scary".   These first two steps are fairly standard clinical protocol for the treatment of nightmares.   The therapist then brings in the television metaphor.   With the client, create a television out of the cardboard box.   Start by cutting out a screen large enough to show the pieces of paper on which the client drew the nightmare. The child is then given the remote control.   Old remote controls at can be found at thrift stores, neighbor's houses.   Places like Target, Wal-Mart and Circuit City may be willing to give you old, extra or broken ones).   The child should get to keep the remote control, take it home and sleep with it.   If actual remote controls are too hard for you to find, you and the child can create your own.   If you choose this route, the therapist and client can customize the remote control.   For example, one button could represent the scary dream "The monster chases me" and another button could represent the alternate dream "The monster sings "Twinkle, Twinkle, little star". Encourage the client to come up with several alternate endings for the dream.   In the above example, the monster sings a child's song instead.   Another ending might be that the child takes on superhuman strength and makes a bolder fall on top of the monster and squashes it flat as a pancake.   Encourage the outrageous.   Make the alternate endings funny or outlandish.   Move behind the T.V. set with all the drawings.   Hold up the nightmare drawing on the screen.

The client uses the remote control and presses a button to "change the channel" while making an empowering statement to the nightmare. Some examples are "get off my screen", "I'm watching something else", etc. The therapist quickly holds up one of the changed images as the child changes the channel.

Processing Questions:
What is the scariest part of your dream?
What part of your changed dream do you like best?
Who is in charge of the remote control?
What are some times when changing the channel could help you?

Homework Assignment:
Take the remote control to bed with you every night this week. Pretend like the T.V. screen is on your wall. You don't have to revisualize the nightmare, but "click" through all of the changed, happy ending dreams that you created before going to sleep each night. Be prepared to talk about your experiences during the next session.

Special Considerations:
Children who are suffering from Post Traumatic Stress Disorder need to have trauma reenactment work and more direct debriefing interventions in addition to metaphoric techniques. The traumatic event engendered the nightmares or flashbacks must be addressed. Moreover, relaxation training and work that helps to ground the client in the here and now must be completed prior to this exercise.

Applications and Modifications: This technique carries
the most power when done one on one with a client. The material can be very scary and the complete attention and support of the therapist will help empower the client generate alternative images. Moreover, when the images are trauma base, the therapist may have to move in and out of relaxation

exercises, free play and reality grounding procedures as the child is triggered. The technique can also *be* effective in a family setting. The parents get insight into the nature of the scary images that their child faces and the parents can help generate replacement images and can lend power and support to changing the channel. Moreover, they can help reinforce the ritual at *bedtime* every night.

Problem Solving and Other Coping Strategies

Dump It On The King

Treatment Modality: Group/Family
Population: Ages 6 to adult
Treatment Phase: Working

Treatment Goals:
1. To practice asking for help
2. To practice problem-solving strategies
3. To receive help with others
4. To increase feelings of hope

Props:
King's (or queen's) crown
scepter
mini trash can
pens
paper

Procedure:
Begin by normalizing the experience of having problems without solutions. Give a couple of examples and talk about how listening to someone wise really helped. Clients are then asked to write down a problem that they don't know what to do about. However, it should be written as a question. Explain that each participant is going to get a chance to be King...They will wear the King's crown, carry the scepter and sit or stand in an elevated position above everyone else. All the questions will be

tossed into the mini trash can. One loyal subject (another group member) will draw a question out of the trash can and "dump it" on the King, who has to come up with a solution. Children love to be put in the role of the expert. A child who cannot come up with a solution to his own problem may be able to think with a different perspective as the "authority" and come up with good advice for someone else. The main rule of the game is that in order to be King, you really have to try to give good advice. A child who gives advice like "go beat him up" will be removed from the throne and may be given another chance to be King later in the game. The other important rule is that group members cannot guess (out loud) about which problem was generated by which group member. The problems should remain anonymous. The layers of removal from the problem really help the child who generated the problem to receive the advice. The child's resistance is down, because he is listening to "the king" give advice to "a subject", not to him. If the King gets stuck, he can choose any group member to become a "royal advisor" and help come up with solutions.

Processing Questions:
What did it feel like to be the King?
What solutions did you come up with as the King...and how did you decide that these would work?
What new ideas did you get about the problem that you dumped on the King?

Homework Assignment:
Try one of the strategies that the King gave you for dealing with your problem. Be prepared to report on how it worked.

Special Considerations:
Children with learning disabilities may have a difficult time with this activity because it requires reading and writing. However, the therapist can fill in the gaps in the writing and reading if necessary. Also, very shy, withdrawn children may refuse to

take a turn as the King, *because* they *do* not want to *be* in the limelight. Allow them to watch the proceedings, *but* they should still generate a problem to dump on the King.

Applications and Modifications:

This technique can *be used* with children who have all kinds of difficulties. If it's a problem and can *be* formed into a question, it can *be* dumped on the King. This technique can also *be* adapted for use in family sessions. Problems that involve the family system can *be* generated and then each family member gets a turn to *be* "king" and generate solutions to the problem.

This technique can also *be* modified and used as a termination activity. If used this way, questions are generated by the therapist and reflect the treatment process. Questions might include, "What *do* children worry about when they first come to therapy?", "What *do* children learn in therapy?", "What's one way children can remember the time spent in therapy?", etc. Each participant gets a turn to *be* the King and share about what he has gained through the treatment process.

Pictured above is one example of a mini trashcan that can *be* used to "Dump It On The King" as well as several variations of crowns for kings and queens. Children can even make their own crowns and take them home after the activity is complete.

Break Down The Walls

Treatment Modality: Group/Family

Population: Ages 5 to adult

Treatment Phase: Working

Treatment Goals:

1. To decrease social isolation
2. To empower client to employ new coping mechanisms
3. To increase client's sense of being supported and socially connected

Props:

plastic sheeting (or)
an old sheet (or)
cling wrap (or)
aluminum foil
paints/markers/etc.

Procedure:

(If you are going to make the wall from scratch, this activity may take two sessions).   The therapist begins by talking about the different kinds of walls that we can build around ourselves...walls of shyness, walls of worry, walls of violence, walls of shame, etc. Several years ago, I came across a

183

prefabricated long plastic "brick" wall. This wall has become a wonderful prop to use in communicating therapeutic metaphors. For this activity, the wall can be made by the group. Plastic sheeting or an old bed sheet can be cut into long strips, these can be attached to each other and painted to reflect a long, low brick wall. The same kind of thing could be done with saran wrap or tinfoil...be creative!! Once the wall is completed, choose one client to stand in the middle and be wrapped up in the wall. The group can choose the kind of wall that the person in the middle has built around himself. For example, if the group decides that the wall is shyness (social isolation). Each group member generates a strategy for the walled-in client to try. This might be asking a peer to come over to play. It might be saying to himself "It's not that they don't like me, they just don't know me yet." Each client gets to tell his strategy to the client wrapped in the wall. If this strategy seems like one that could work, the client who came up with the idea gets to unwrap a section of the wall from around the client. The activity continues until the group has torn down the wall completely and the walled-in client is free.

Processing Questions:
What did it feel like to be walled in? Was it hard to move? To communicate? How so?
What were some of the ideas that your friends came up with to help get you out?
How did it feel to be unwrapped?
What was it like to get to help unwrap your friend?
What is the most helpful strategy that your friends came up with?
How can you use this in your life?

Homework Assignment:
Before your next visit, use one of the ideas that helped break down your wall in one real life situation that you face. Be ready to tell us all about it!

Special Considerations:

Children who are survivors of abuse may not want to be wrapped up in the wall. Honor their boundaries and allow them to be helpers for the whole of the game. They may decide, through watching the others get wrapped up and then unwrapped, that they want to try it. Either way, they still benefit from all the brainstorming that happens related to coping strategies.

Applications and Modifications:

This technique yields the maximum therapeutic benefits when it is done in a group setting. Clients are using their problem solving skills to help one another as well as increase their own arsenals of coping strategies. The client who is wrapped in the wall gets the experience of being physically released by supportive people who desire for him to be free. Then that client gets to help others be freed. Meantime, everyone is generating and practicing creative strategies for coping with the problems of life. Fully unwrapping one client may take an entire session. In order for all clients to get a turn to be the walled-in person, the therapist may want to plan five to six group sessions with walls at the center of the curriculum. A different therapeutic topic can be chosen for each week and represented by a wall. For example, one week could be about how to tear down the wall of anger that we can build around ourselves (anger management strategies would be generated). The next week could be about how to tear down a wall of worries (anxiety reduction strategies would be generated).

This technique can also be adapted to use with families but the wall could be used more as a metaphor for maintaining healthy boundaries between people. For example, in a structural family therapy approach, family members may be asked to wall themselves in with the person they feel closest to. Help them process the pros and cons of being so tightly bonded with each other as the wall is loosened from around them.

Ultimately, the wall will not *be* completely wrapped around anyone, *but* can function as a low healthy *boundary* line that delineates one family member from another.

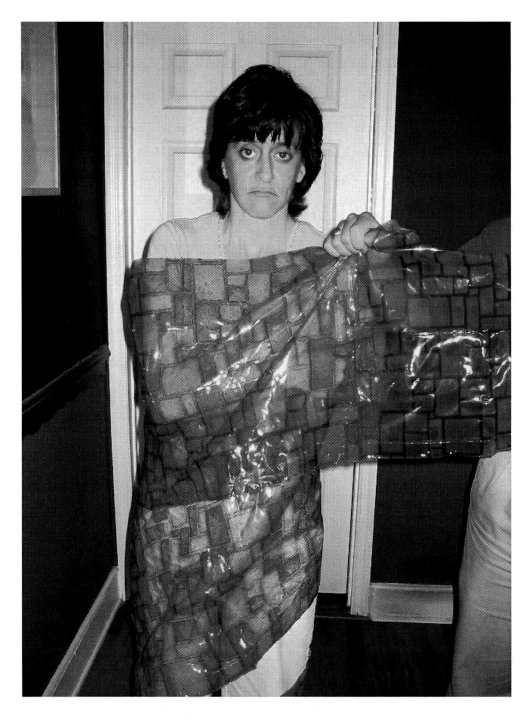

In the above picture, the wall *being* unwrapped from around the player is made of plastic sheeting.

Singing in the Rain

Treatment Modality: Individual/Group/Family
Population: Ages 5 to adult
Treatment Phase: Working

Treatment Goals:

1. To recognize oncoming symptoms of depression,
2. To identify coping strategies to ward off depression
3. To replace negative self-talk statements with positive ones
4. To empower the client to "protect" herself from spiraling into depression

Props:

a multi-colored umbrella or umbrella hat
a permanent black marker

Procedure:

Begin by comparing depression to a heavy rain. The client may believe that everything is going well and then all of a sudden she feels depressed. The comparison between a rainstorm and depression can help her understand that warning signs do exist, if one knows how to look for them. Explain to the client, "If you're busy doing other things, you make look out the window and suddenly realize that it's pouring down rain. However, if you had been actively looking for the signs, you might have noticed the air becoming more humid, the sky darkening, and thunder rumbling in the distance...or you might have turned on the news and had a weatherperson tell you that the rain would soon be coming. Depression works the same way. Think back over the previous times that you've gotten depressed...what starts to happen to you? What starts to happen around you?" The client may need lots of help from the therapist in describing the downward spiral, but the list may include some of the following:

1) Wanting to sleep all the time
2) Having trouble focusing in class and completing assignment,
3) Saying negative things to yourself about yourself,
4) Not eating properly,
5) Not spending as much time with friends

The client may be surprised to recognize these signs. Return to the rainstorm metaphor. "If you don't see the rain coming, you can't prepare for it so you get caught out in the rain and soaked to the skin. If you knew the rain was coming, what would you do?" Most clients will answer that they would stay inside or use an umbrella. The therapist then produces the small, brightly colored umbrella that will become the client's "protection" from the rainstorms (depression) in his life. The umbrella has stripes of color running from the top of the umbrella down the sides...there are usually at least five or six stripes of color. The client is going to write a coping strategy in each stripe of color. For example, one stripe might say "spend time with friends", another might say "take medicine regularly", another might say "eat healthy", etc. The specific coping strategies may vary from client to client, but in most cases the components of a healthy lifestyle should make the list.

188

Processing Questions:

What are some of your warning signs that depression might be coming?

Do you have a choice in whether or not depression soaks you? Why or why not?

What are some of the strategies that will help you avoid getting soaked?

How will you use this umbrella?

Homework Assignment:

Pick one of the coping strategies written on your umbrella and implement it every day this week. If you choose the "eat healthy" strategy, you must eat three square meals a day. You get to choose which strategy to use this week. Be ready to report on how it goes.

Special Considerations:

For any child who is dealing with a serious depression, the therapist must assess for suicidal ideation and have the client sign a "no-harm" contract. A psychiatric evaluation for the possible use of medication is also advisable previous to the implementation of behavioral training. Preschool age children may not have the ability to engage in the meta-analysis that is necessary to notice patterns that lead up to depressed feelings. With young children, you could compare the way that the umbrella protects the client from the rain to the way that mommy or daddy will protect the client from acting on sad feelings if the client will use her words to tell the caregiver how she is feeling.

Applications and Modifications:

The metaphor of protection from an imminent danger or discomfort by the umbrella full of coping tools can be adapted to many different situations. Positive self-talk statements could be written on the umbrella and figuratively held up to ward off the negative messages sent by peers. Strategies for increasing the likelihood that a child will not *be* physically or sexually abused again can *be* written on the umbrella and practiced. Strategies for reducing and managing anger can *be* written on the umbrella as protection from violent outbursts that end in trouble for the client. The list goes on and on. The technique could also *be* used during the termination phase to review some of the strategies for healthy living that the child has learned in therapy. Writing them on the umbrella and giving the umbrella to the child will send the message "I trust you to take care of yourself and get the help you need when you need it." This technique can also *be* used in group. Each participant can have their own umbrella, or the group could use a larger umbrella that will stay in the room as a ever-present prop and reminder of the ways in which they can protect themselves from the things life throws at them.

The umbrella pictured above includes many of the coping strategies that clients suffering from depression can use to increase health. Two of the patches of color have been left blank, because each client will need to generate some strategies that are unique to his particular situation or life stressors.

Lose the Bruise

Treatment Modality: Individual/Group
Population: Ages 5 to adult
Treatment Phase: Working

Treatment Goals:

1. To identify and verbalize ways in which the client has been emotionally or physically hurt
2. To develop coping strategies for dealing with the hurts
3. To practice, through role play, the strategies for quick implementation when needed

Props:

small balls with feeling faces (and bruises or bandaids on them)
plastic sword
plastic shield
plastic helmet

Procedure:

Begin by showing the kick balls to the client and comparing their bruises and scrapes to the bruises and scrapes that we receive when we are hurt by other people's words and actions. For each bruised kickball, the client and therapist make up a story about how the kickball got that bruise. Steer some of the stories to physical bruises and some to emotional bruises. An example story follows: "This kickball asked to play soccer with some of the other kickballs at school and they laughed at him and told him he was too much of a loser to play." The therapist writes out the scenario for each kickball. After all the bruises have been accounted for, introduce the idea of deflecting the hurts before they get a chance to cause bruises. Explain that the client can develop certain strategies that will deflect the hurts that other people (particularly peers) may try to throw at him. These strategies might include positive self-talk, exercising more wisdom in who he asks to play with, finding adults to support and encourage him, laughing off the comments of peers, etc. It is critical that the client help to generate the particular strategies that will make sense in his world, or he will not buy into the therapeutic process. The client and therapist then role play each of the scenarios that were written in the stories earlier. The therapist plays the part of the peer who is trying to hurt the client (with words or fists). Throw the bruised kickball (as a metaphor for the hurt) towards the client while making a hurtful statement or action. The client is given the sword and the shield. His job is to deflect the hurt by practicing one of the coping strategies as he bats the kickball away. This technique is especially effective with school age boys, who find the prospect of using the warrior props and hitting the kickballs very appealing.

Processing Questions:

What are the different ways in which we can be hurt?
Could you see the hurts coming?
What did you have to do to ward them off?
Which of your coping strategies felt the most natural to you?
When are some times in your life when using the coping strategies can deflect hurts?

Homework Assignment:

Pick the coping strategy that felt most natural to you. During the coming week, try to see the hurts coming and use this strategy to deflect them. Before you go to bed each night, take a minute to visualize the shield you used in the playroom. Imagine using it in different situations that came up during your day.

Special Considerations:

Clients who have difficulty with pretend play may have a hard time "playing along with" the therapist as she communicates the hurtful words or situations to the client. They may feel that the therapist is no longer on their side. Be aware of this possibility and be prepared to substitute a puppet (preferably one that looks like a bully) as the aggressor who throws the hurts at the client.

Applications and Modifications:

This technique is used mainly to help clients generate and practice coping skills. However, the content of the "scrapes and bruises" is highly adaptable. The hurtful material that the client is learning to fight can run the gambit from verbal abuse to bullying to grief and loss issues. This technique is easily adaptable to a group setting. In this case, each participant would be given one of the kickballs and asked to create a story about how that kickball got hurt. Then that client tries to "throw" the hurt at another group member who must deflect it (after the group has generated helpful strategies).

The above picture shows one kind of kickball that can be used to show the bruises. Below the kickballs are listed some of the "word bruises" that peers try to throw at clients.

Wisdom Feathers

Treatment Modality: Individual/Group/Family
Population: Ages 5 to adult
Treatment Phase: Beginning/Working/Termination

Treatment Goals:

1. To develop problem solving skills
2. To practice problem solving skills for quick implementation when needed
3. To enhance self-esteem through being useful to the group

Props:

clay
brightly colored feathers
one set of large googly eyes
owl puppet (hand or finger)

Procedure:

Begin by talking about owls and how wise they are. Explain to the client that owls live in the forest and all the little animals, when they have problems, go ask the owl's help in figuring out what to do. Explain to the client that although she can't take a trip all the way out to the forest every time she has a problem, she can create her own owl to keep here in the playroom. That way, she can ask its advice whenever she needs help. Since the owl is being made from scratch, we're going to make its' body and cover it with feathers. Since it will be a brand new owl, it will even have to be given its' wisdom. The group will make the owl's body out of clay, and attach large googly eyes and a beak. Explain that each client will get a turn to pretend to be the owl (the client can use the owl puppet during her turn). Another group member will think of a problem that "a lot of children have trouble with" and the client playing the part of the owl will have to come up with at least one solution to the problem. These solutions can even be written down and "stored" inside the hollowed out owl. Problem solving steps can be listed near the group and the owl can either generate the solution or help the group member with the problem to work through the steps. Whenever a reasonable solution to the problem is generated, the client gets to add a feather to the owl, by sticking the plume into the clay. The owl may not get completed in one session, but a process for working through problem solving steps will have been set up. In future group session, when a client has a problem, the therapist can bring out the owl and the feathers and continue to let the group feather the owl through every problem solving session.

Processing Questions:
List the steps of the problem solving process.
Which step is the easiest for you?
Which step is the hardest?
What is one helpful suggestion that the owl made to help you deal with your problem?

Homework Assignment:
Try out the suggestion that the owl gave you. Report back on how it worked.

Special Considerations:

Some clients may be so new to the problem solving process that they aren't able to get past looking at the problem. In these cases, feathers could be awarded for each step that is completed...so that if all the client can do is define the problem, she gets a feather. If she completes three steps of the process, she gets to add three feathers, etc.

Applications and Modifications:

The main purpose of the technique is to serve as a vehicle for training clients to implement the problem solving process. It can, therefore, be adapted to serve whatever client population you work with, from ADD children to children suffering from Bipolar Disorder. Although the technique is designed for group implementation, you could create a mini-owl for individual clients and use the technique in that setting. Another interesting way to use this technique would be in family work. You can help the family create a wise owl that they can take home with them and put in the middle of the table during family meetings to remind them to use the steps of the problem solving process that they were trained in as a family.

References
and recommended readings

Accorsi, William.   (1999).   *10 Button Book.*   New York: Workman Publishing.

Boyd-Webb, Nancy.   (1991).   *Play Therapy with Children in Crisis: A Casebook for Practitioners.*   New York: Guilford Press.

Carle, Eric.   (1996).   *Little Cloud.*   New York: Philomel Books.

Carle, Eric.   (1990).   *The Very Quiet Cricket.*   New York: Philomel Books.

Curtis, Jamie Lee.   (2000)   *Where Do Balloons Go? An Uplifting Mystery.*   New York: Joanne Cotler Books.

Davis, Nancy, PhD.   (1996).   *Once Upon a Time...Therapeutic Stories that Teach and Heal.*   Distributed by the Self-Esteem Shop.

Gil, Eliana.   (1994).   *Play in Family Therapy.*   New York: Guilford Press.

Gil, Eliana.   (1991).   *The Healing Powers of Play: Working with Abused Children.*   New York: Guilford Press.

James, Beverly.   (1989).   *Treating Traumatized Children: New Insights and Creative Interventions.*   New York: The Free Press.

Knell, S.   (1993).   *Cognitive-Behavioral Play Therapy.*   New Jersey: Jason Aronson.

Kubler-Ross, Elisabeth, M.D.   (1969).   *On Death and Dying.*   New York: Touchstone.

O'Conner, Kevin J.   (1983).   The Color Your Life Technique. In C.E. Schaefer & K.J. O'Connor (Eds), *Handbook of Play Therapy.*   New York: John Wiley & Sons.

Ransom, Jeanie Franz.   (2000)   I Don't Want to Talk About It.   Magination Publishers.

Shaw, Charles G.   (1947),   *It Looked Like Spilt Milk.*   Harper Festival Publishers.

Sweeney, Daniel S. and Homeyer, Linda E. (Eds.)   (1999).   *The Handbook of Group Play Therapy: How to Do it, How it Works, Whom it's Best for.*   San Fransisco: Jossey-Bass, Inc.